CANTERBURY PILGRIM

Also by Michael Ramsey
published by SPCK
The Christian Priest Today
Freedom, Faith and the Future

Canterbury Pilgrim

MICHAEL RAMSEY

LONDON
SPCK
1974

First published in 1974
Second impression 1974
SPCK
Holy Trinity Church
Marylebone Road
London NW1 4DU

Printed in Great Britain by
The Camelot Press Ltd, Southampton

SBN 281 02810 9

Contents

Illustrations

Acknowledgements

Thanks are due to the following for permission to quote from copyright sources:

Harvard University Press: *The Feast of Fools*, by Harvey Cox

Hutchinson & Co. Ltd: *The Life of Henry Herbert Asquith*, by J. A. Spender and Cyril Asquith

Sheed and Ward, Inc.: *Is the Last Supper Finished?*, by Arthur Vogel

Preface

This book contains addresses and lectures given in the last few years of my time as Archbishop of Canterbury, together with a preliminary chapter called 'Lessons of a Pilgrimage' which suggests the motive of the book.

I have named the book *Canterbury Pilgrim*, for while my office has been that of a teacher of the Christian faith I have found myself a learner amidst the changing and unpredictable scenes of the 1960s and after. In the world there has been the increase of violence, the polarizing of racial conflict, the confusion of morals, and the sharpened awareness of the contrast between the affluent and the hungry peoples. In Christendom there has been the theological malaise associated with the phrase 'Death of God', the decline of church allegiance, the revivals of a charismatic kind, the involvement of Christianity with the problems of social revolution, and the growing feeling in the West for prayer and contemplation as essential to the life of Man. Who would have foreseen the renewal within the Roman Catholic Church during and after the Second Vatican Council, or the startling advances and frustrations in the ecumenical scene? Through these bewildering years I have tried to learn, as only a learning Church can be a Church which guides.

The essay on 'Church and State in England' was newly written for this volume. With a few exceptions, none of the pieces has appeared in print before. I am grateful for permission to reprint the Gore Lecture on 'The Historical Jesus' (*Theology*) and the articles on 'The Meaning of Life' (*Sunday Times*) and 'Christ and Humanism' (*Spectator*). A number of pieces are concerned with Christology, for it seems that Christology is returning to the centre of the scene of theological interest and the Person of Jesus Christ is stirring many people beyond as well as within the Churches. We need not be obsessed by the fortunes of Christian institutions if our concern is about Jesus Christ, the same yesterday, today, and for ever, himself the Lord, the Judge, and the Renewer of the Church.

I thank my secretary, Miss Barbara Lepper, for her great help in the preparation of this and other of my works in recent years.

As I approach the end of my Canterbury pilgrimage I would express my gratitude to those in many countries who have helped me by their encouragement, their actions, and their prayers. Saying goodbye to any share in the Church's government and policies, I would try to continue my pilgrimage with those who believe, in the words which Thomas Becket chose as the text of one of his last sermons in his Cathedral, that 'we have here no continuing city'.

MICHAEL CANTUAR:

Lessons of a Pilgrimage

Lessons of a Pilgrimage

The sixties and early seventies of this century have seen in Christendom shocks, surprises, and ups and downs in plenty, and history will one day have much to say about them in a perspective which is not yet to be had. I record here three of the impressions which have been specially vivid on my own journey through this period as a Canterbury pilgrim, and I try to draw such lessons as I can. The impressions concern a crisis of faith, a renewal of religion, and a big shift in the map of Christendom in the world.

At the beginning of the sixties there was in the Church of England little awareness that a theological upheaval was on its way. The revision of the Church's Canon Law had been a prolonged and absorbing task, with the belief that the provision of an up-to-date law for the Church would assist efficiency in the work of the gospel. But there were some who realized that urgent questions about the nature and the presentation of the Christian faith were near at hand. This concern was seen in the volume called *Soundings* which came from Cambridge in 1962. Its authors probed into some of the questions but shrank from any comprehensive 'restatement' in the belief that the time for this was not yet ready.

For my own part, I was aware that the 'biblical theology' within whose stream most of my own theological work had been done was in danger of talking in a vacuum unrelated to the world around. But the lack of a common 'universe of discourse' made impossible that Christian 'map' of the world, with the Incarnation at the centre, of which William Temple had dreamed in his earlier writings. Not believing that a logical or philosophical synthesis of Christianity and contemporary modes of thought was possible, I none the less believed, as I still do, that the death and resurrection of Jesus Christ give through faith some shape and clue to the meaning of existence. As one whose theology had been almost entirely 'historical' in discipline, I thought that the Christian tradition had within itself resources of supernatural faith and spirituality equal to whatever shocks might come.

The storm over *Honest to God* broke in March 1963. I was at the time, after eighteen strenuous months in finding my feet in a new office, scarcely prepared for a theological crisis. The initial error in reaction, in which I myself shared, was to think that the trouble was only that the author of the book was missing some of the profundities of the Christian faith and was being unnecessarily negative in expression. I think that was true. But I was soon to grasp how many were the contemporary gropings and quests which lay behind *Honest to God*. Again, I rather supposed that the need was to reaffirm the coherence of the faith on familiar lines, albeit with greater sensitivity and persuasion. If that was my initial mistake, I saw after a little further reflection that there was in the background a widespread crisis of faith which cried out for another kind of spirit in meeting it. I thus described this spirit, and if my words sounded at all new in the contemporary Anglican scene they were in line with not a few of the Anglican teachers of the past:

> Since the war our Church has been too inclined to be concerned with the organising of its own life, perhaps assuming too easily that the faith may be taken for granted and needs only to be stated and commended. But we state and commend the faith only in so far as we go out and put ourselves with loving sympathy inside the doubts of the doubting, the questions of the questioners, and the loneliness of those who have lost their way.[1]

What had been happening? English theology has often been very insular and unaware of trends on the continent of Europe. The bomb which exploded in 1963 therefore caused the more consternation in that it included, condensed within a single packet, the quintessence of three divines as un-English as they were different from one another: Tillich, Bonhoeffer, and Bultmann. Tillich's substitution of the language of 'ground of our being' for the familiar imagery of theism, Bonhoeffer's thesis of 'Christianity without religion', Bultmann's view that the gospel is an existentialist encounter with Jesus without the

[1] *Image Old and New* (London 1963), p. 14.

framework of earth and heaven and without the pattern of his historical career—all these themes appeared in one package. These revolutions might perhaps have been digested one at a time with the dilution and the finesse with which English minds can sometimes absorb new and foreign conceptions. But, coming all of a sudden and coming all together within the covers of a single paperback, Tillich, Bultmann, and Bonhoeffer made an explosion which could be heard.

The explosion, however, while it distressed many of the faithful for whom we must care, was not unrelated to gropings, conscious and unconscious, which had been widespread amongst many people on the periphery of faith. There were those to whom the imagery of God on a throne in heaven (imagery which they may never have heard paraphrased intelligently) was wearisome, while they warmed to the idea that something deep within themselves had transcendent significance. There were those who had learned from Jesus that God is the God of the market place as well as the temple, and had wondered whether the God of 'churchy' people was the same God. There were those who understood the meaning of an existential encounter with Jesus (though they would never use that language), and—however wrongly—felt encumbered by what seemed to be the load of myth and miracle. In fact a world of half-belief and half-doubt, of searchings and questionings, was being dug up by *Honest to God*. What was the orthodox teacher to do? He could show, I think with some truth, that in the Robinson thesis negative inferences seemed to be unduly emphasized and that orthodoxy was sometimes caricatured. But here was the opportunity to learn from that wistful world which was being uncovered, to understand, to discriminate, and then to try to guide with patience.

It soon was clear that *Honest to God* was only an item in a larger scene. There were other books and other excitements which illustrated the crisis of faith. I do not discuss here the 'Death of God' concepts, partly because I have done so before,[1] and partly because these concepts now seem to belong to the past. But I mention a sad aspect of the malaise of faith: it coincided with a malaise concerning prayer and worship. It has been held

[1] Cf. *God, Christ and the World*. London 1969; *The Christian Priest Today* (London 1972), ch. 5.

to be one of the characteristics of Anglicanism that the tradition of prayer and worship intermingles with the work of theology, preaching, and practical service. The *lex orandi* has for us been felt to underlie the *lex credendi*. So it has sometimes happened that in times of intellectual disturbance, criticism, and change, when negatives tend to be prominent, the tradition of prayer and worship has kept alive the sense of Creator and creature, Saviour and sinner, as the heart of what is essentially Christian. The sadness of the sixties was that the shocks of faith synchronized with the querying of the practice of the spiritual life.

The querying of spirituality had its remoter and its nearer causes. There had been the long trend towards social activism in the Christianity of the West, and the reaction against 'pietism'. There was the growing urge to find transcendence through the world rather than away from it. Already present on the scene, the 'non-prayer' tendency was heightened by the specific notions of secular Christianity as epitomized, for instance, in Harvey Cox's *The Secular City*.[1] And amongst those who valued prayer there were some inhibiting ideas, like the idea that a 'going apart' is to be deprecated as escapism—which meant being wiser than our Lord who was found by Simon Peter praying alone in a desert place a great while before day.

These were some of the ingredients in the crisis of faith which loomed so large in the sixties. Faced by all this, there were many in the Church of England who found themselves burdened and embarrassed. A tendency came for theology to be polarized between those who were influenced by the new ideas and those who turned to an authoritarian and conservative biblical theology offering a security of faith which could sometimes include elements of fear and a failure to face the questionings of the mind. It was a test for 'leadership'. There were those who exhorted the faithful to be true to the gospel, lamented that these troubles had made the task of the Christian preacher difficult, and said in effect 'please do not rock the boat'. There were those, and would that there had been more of them, who tried to combine a hold upon the deep values of tradition with a sensitive understanding of the turmoil. Questions needed to be faced, and need to be faced still. How far is a lifeless and undynamic use of religious imagery responsible for misunderstanding of theism?

[1] London 1965.

How far does a tendency to exalt Jesus while professing to reject theism call for a deeper grasp of the Christlikeness of God amongst his exponents? May the negative concept of a religionless Christianity be redeemed into the positive theme of a lay spirituality?

These are real questions, and they are with us still. The lessons of the crisis of faith may have helped us and may help us still to know the glory of the Triune God, the Creator, the Judge, and the Saviour of Man, and to proclaim it with more humility, more love, and more understanding of those who find faith hard. O passi graviora, it is through the facing of dark nights, whether in the mystery of God or in the agonies of the world, that the deepening of faith is realized.

As he walks on from the sixties towards the mid-seventies, this Canterbury pilgrim begins to find himself in a different scene and a different climate. The apathy about God and Christianity remains, morals are even more chaotic, and the world is even more cruel. Nor is the dislike of 'institutions' any less. But amongst the faithful there is a lively faith, worship has a greater 'boldness of access', and the loss of nerve seems to belong to yesterday. The pilgrim sees more often not the spectre of atheism within the Church but powerful movements of spirituality of one kind and another, some without and some within the Churches, and his problem is what to do and to say about these.

'Death of God' belongs to the past. I sense that in the realm of theology it is Christology which is returning to the centre. This may be partly because Jesus Movements, both popular and academic, are making themselves felt. But I think it is partly also because for theism itself the question of the Christlikeness of God has come to the fore, as well as the exploration of how far the death and resurrection of Jesus Christ is the clue to the sovereignty of God and to Man's hope for himself and the world. Christ, Hope, Resurrection are increasingly the themes of theology today.

Not surprisingly the present book contains no essays on the 'Death of God', but I include several pieces about Christology. In one of them I express the conviction that the framework in which the early Church understood Jesus Christ was less the framework of a local earth below and a local heaven above than the framework of Creator and creature, Saviour and sinner.

Bc

It is perhaps in this area that we may see the line of difference between the faith of the Incarnation and reductionist ideas which miss its depth.

'Charismatic' revival is seen not only in sects and in the organized Pentecostal Churches but within Anglican and Roman Catholic Churches, bringing liveliness and renewal. I am very critical of the concept of 'baptism' which is often invoked, as I believe it to rest upon misleading interpretation of the New Testament. I share the concern of others that the Spirit's *charismata* are many and diverse and that none may rightly be singled out as the criterion of the Spirit's presence. But the liveliness of the Holy Spirit is indeed apparent in new ways. The Jesus Movements also are only a part of the wider phenomenon of the return of religion in many ways and in many scenes.

Prayer and worship are deepening in Western Christianity. The Harvey Cox of *The Secular City* has become the Harvey Cox of *The Feast of Fools*. Social activism finds its territory invaded by neo-mysticism. Christians are asking what they may be learning from Zen and Yoga. In England many are learning about prayer from contemporary writers as different as Archbishop Bloom and Monica Furlong. The kind of audiences which a few years ago might have asked me to address them about race or social action nowadays often ask to be addressed about prayer. But I have seldom sensed an escape from the world as the motive of this new spiritual hunger, for often the stream of desire for 'contemplation' and the stream of concern for social justice flow together. Amongst young people, Taizé illustrates this confluence of the streams in an impressive way. There, the Religious Community has its Brothers working in a variety of secular employments in the neighbourhood and joining thrice daily in the offices of worship in the Community Church. And nearby there are through the year thousands of young people in camps, coming from many countries. Their talk is of the fight for social justice in their own countries, and with no sense of irrelevance they join three times a day in the worship of the Community with its ample provision of silence. 'Contemplation' is the word in use, and it is this which draws them.[1]

---

[1] The word 'contemplation' is often used today not of the particular phenomenon described by mystical writers as 'contemplative prayer' but of

The revival of religion in the West is a wide and very varied phenomenon, and it cannot be contained within descriptions of 'the religions'. Amidst the pressures and strains of life there is the longing of the self to realize itself in freedom from the dominance of time and environment. Many cults, and some drugs, offer the promise of this freedom; but there is a difference between a freedom which may be no more than 'the shortest way out of Manchester' and a freedom whereby the self finds the vigorous peace of moral energy. Religion is itself a neutral phenomenon, and like everything else it needs to be redeemed. Nothing matters more than that the reviving religious awareness in the West should be met by a Christianity, and not least by a Christian priesthood, which knows its own mystical tradition and can guide religion to move along the way of Christ.

Within the Churches of the West, Liturgy is reviving, and Roman Catholics, Anglicans, Reformed Christians, and others are experiencing its revival. I am thinking of something deeper than the revision of forms of worship or the questions about archaic and modern language. For centuries in the West Liturgy was apt to be something for the faithful to *attend*. But in truth Liturgy is something for the faithful to *do*; and it is the realization of this which has been changing the church life of many parts of Christendom. Liturgy embraces both at its periphery the human concept of 'celebrating' and at its centre the memorial of the sacrifice of Christ in his death, resurrection, and ascension. In obedience to Christ we take, we break, we offer, we receive; and Christ makes accessible to us his own self-offering into which we are drawn. Liturgy gathers into one the 'contemplation' of God in Christ and the mission of Christian people in the re-creation of the world. Feeding upon him they become again his body through which he is working for the refashioning of the world. Liturgy is thus the true place of confluence of the stream of contemplation and the stream of outgoing service in the world.

The Canterbury pilgrim rejoices to have seen the Church of England use its powers for liturgical reform in recent years in

---

all prayer in which there is quiet attention and waiting upon God. There is also, however, a revival of contemplative prayer in the stricter sense, within the Religious Life and elsewhere.

such a way as to help the people with greater understanding to *do* the liturgy and to *be* the Church. The Series 2 service did much to recover the pattern of liturgical action, and it has enabled churchmen of different schools of thought to share joyfully in one rite. The Series 3 service has added a true liveliness of language, but some confusion in sacrificial language (due to a strange reversion to sixteenth-century concepts) needs to be removed before this rite can become the final product of revision for the seventies and beyond.

My pilgrimage through the crisis of faith and the revivals of religion perforce leads me far beyond the scene of England or Europe or the West, for faith is in the God of the whole suffering world, and religious revival is, as we have seen, inter-mingled with issues of justice and human brotherhood. So I turn to some of the lessons of the ecumenical scene, and of the world around it.

Setting out to use my office in the service of the ecumenical cause, I saw the task on the familiar and predictable lines of theological synthesis and the bringing of Churches into communion with one another on the principle of the Lambeth Quadrilateral of creed, scripture, sacraments, and episcopate. I was specially eager that progress with the Orthodox East, long delayed by political causes, should be resumed, and the series of visits which I made to the Patriarchates bore fruit in the creation of the Anglican–Orthodox Theological Commission which, after long preparation, had its first full meeting at Oxford in 1973. But how unpredictable was Rome! Who foresaw the renewal associated with the Second Vatican Council with its repercussions for the life of Christendom? No Canterbury pilgrim had dreamed that in March 1966 a Pope and an Arch-bishop would publicly sign in the Basilica of St Paul-without-the-Walls the Common Declaration asking the two Communions to engage in 'a serious dialogue based upon the Holy Gospels and ancient common traditions'; or that the ensuing joint Theological Commission would produce the Agreed Statement on the Eucharist (1971) and the Agreed Statement on Ministry and Ordination (1973). The journey now approaches the more difficult terrain.

Nor have ecumenical happenings in England followed predictable lines. Previously wedded to ideas of federation combined with intercommunion, the Free Churches have moved in thought towards the quest of organic union in one Church, and the Anglican–Methodist dialogue accordingly moved beyond the idea of full communion to the necessity of one Church as the 'second stage'. The failure of the Church of England to accept in 1972 the proposals for full communion with the Methodists, which the Methodists had twice endorsed, robbed the Church of England of credible initiative in relation to the Free Churches. Meanwhile there came in 1972 the inauguration of the United Reformed Church and its subsequent initiative in inviting discussion about the possibility of a wider United Church in England. In this volume, while there are many references to the ecumenical scene, I include two pieces specially devoted to it. One is a speech commending the Anglican–Methodist proposals in 1972, for though the scheme is now dead there were issues of truth and integrity which have continuing importance. The other is a lecture in Cambridge dealing with the 'new' ecumenical phase, in which there are the themes of 'non-institutional' Christianity and of the Churches working together to heal the wounds of human injustice.

It is difficult to have a share in the wide-ranging work of Christian unity without realizing that the focus of Christianity in the world has already become no longer Western or white as regards numbers and is becoming no longer Western or white in leadership. And the ethos of the younger Christianity is inevitably different from the ethos of the older. Just as we in the West understand our Christianity through the medium of our Western culture, so inevitably the peoples of the Third World will understand their Christianity through the medium of their own concerns. And their concerns are poverty and the struggle for justice.

It is here that the relations of the older and the younger Christianity are exposed to misunderstandings, amidst the problems of violence and social justice. Some of those problems are discussed in the lecture on Christianity and Violence included in this book. It is rightly pointed out by biblical scholars that the liberation of mankind which Christ brings through the gospel is something deeper and wider than contemporary theologies of liberation sometimes suggest, for its essence is not the substitution of one social order for another but the bringing of Man himself into union with God in eternal life. Nevertheless Christianity is inevitably rejected if its exponents appear to stand on the side of privilege and injustice; and for the Church to be one with those who are oppressed is a part of its mission to be with the people where they are, with them and among them. Only thus is the Church of Christ able credibly to witness that here we have no continuing city.

1

Things that are not Shaken

The Apostolic Age and Our Own

It is with much diffidence that I address this Congress of learned students of the New Testament[1] as it is now more than twenty years since I left the field of academic study and entered the hazardous life of what is called a church leader. However, I accepted the invitation to give this lecture in the belief that for the understanding of the gospel of Jesus Christ and its presentation in any phase of history the role of the historian or the theologian is never wholly separate from the role of the pastor and the evangelist.

This was conspicuously true in the apostolic age. What factors were involved in the understanding of Jesus Christ and in the spread of that understanding in the first Christian century? There was the preaching of good news concerning his death and resurrection, his bestowal of the Holy Spirit and his future coming in glory. There was the handing down by catechists of traditions of what he had said and done in Galilee and Judea. There were sacramental rites in which the members of the Church believed themselves to be united to Jesus as one who died and was alive among them. There was the continuing community of Christians spread in many countries, a community to whom Jesus was the dominant name both for the lives they were expected to live and for the goal to which they looked forward. But the time was short. A note of urgency never ceased to sound. In F. C. Burkitt's words: 'Christianity was from the first organized for a time of catastrophe.' The message must without delay be carried to all the nations. In such an atmosphere there was no room for leisurely research into the remarkable history which had brought the new faith into existence, or for leisurely reflection about its implications for human thought. Yet in the midst of this missionary urgency and pressure an immense intellectual activity was taking place, and Christian theology was being born.

[1] Inaugural Address at the Congress on Biblical Studies at Oxford, 3 September 1973.

Christian theology possessed from the first a book of scriptures regarded as sacred and authoritative, the collection which came to be known to Christians as the Old Testament. This was because Jesus was held to be the Christ, a name which linked him inseparably with the particular history of the Jews and with the God of the Jews who was his God and Father. The first Christians were not indeed the only Jews who used the old scriptures in a new and creative way, bringing their message 'up to date' and interpreting them for new times. In Alexandria Philo had done this by an adventurous exegesis which found in the scriptures anticipations of Greek philosophy and so gave the scriptures a new missionary outreach into the Gentile world. In Palestine the rabbis had done this by their massive use of 'tradition' which enabled the scriptures to give fresh guidance for a hundred and more contemporary problems. But the rabbis could do this, on their own principles, only by a theory of an unwritten tradition of teaching which went back to Moses himself, for Moses must not be superseded. How different was the Christians' use of the Old Testament. For them the scriptures became contemporary and alive because the clue to them was a *contemporary set of events* and a contemporary person who was the subject of those events: Jesus. In his words and works, death and rising again, the things spoken about in the Old Testament— kingdom, king, messiah, peace, mercy, righteousness, exodus, temple, glory—have now happened, and happened in a way that makes the previous occurrence of them only a pale shadow or foretaste. Thus in the Christian Church the authority of the old scriptures was not discarded but enhanced. But it was an authority seen in a new way: the authority of their witness to Christ who was their goal. This witness to Christ was drawn out sometimes in terms of details which may seem to us to be trivial and artificial, sometimes in terms of the broad biblical themes. But the important point is well put by C. K. Barrett: 'The fulfilment is determined by that which fulfils, not by that which is fulfilled.'

The faith that Jesus was the Christ spread rapidly from Palestine into the Graeco-Roman world. Because the gospel implied immense claims for the relations of Jesus to God, to mankind and to the world, it was inevitable that the missionaries and teachers would find varieties of imagery and thought-form to express the meaning of Jesus. Hence there came about varieties of theological expression in different cultural settings. We see the different theological styles in, for instance, the Matthaean Gospel, the Lucan writings, the Epistle to the Hebrews, and the Johannine books. But amidst all the variety there was one unchanging framework. This framework can be described simply: God created the world and mankind; mankind is fallen and sinful; Jesus Christ brings deliverance to the sinful human race; deliverance is into union with Jesus Christ both in this world and beyond it. It is not too much to say that this pattern was invariable as the framework of apostolic belief and teaching, with the duality of Creator and creature, Saviour and sinner. In Jesus the Creator of the world had been at work for the deliverance of mankind, and union with Jesus is the goal into which mankind is delivered.

It is a mistake to think that the duality in early Christianity was primarily the duality of a heaven beyond the sky and an earth here below, though that was the cosmogony of the day and it had its influence upon religious imagery. No, the duality inherent in Christianity from the start was not just the duality of Ptolemaic astronomy, it was the duality between Creator and creature. It was in that context that the meaning of Jesus was understood. One with mankind in their creatureliness, he none the less reveals the Creator to the created world and evokes the worship which creatures can without idolatry give only to their Creator. Similarly Jesus is the source and giver of righteousness to a race stricken with sin and guilt, and the goal into which he delivers the race is a sharing in his own righteousness and perfection. Remove the duality of Creator and creature, righteous Saviour and sinner, and the pattern of primitive Christian theology disappears.

Between the Christianity of the first century and the Christianity of every subsequent age, including our own, there is this significant difference. The apostolic age knew no Canon of the New Testament and no corpus of sacred scriptures other than the Old Testament. Subsequently there came into being the New Testament Canon and its immense authority through the Christian centuries. This has brought both gain and loss. By the existence of the New Testament Canon the unique importance of the apostolic age has been upheld, and the unique significance of the witness of the apostles to Jesus Christ. But there have resulted the inevitable drawbacks which accompany the idea of a 'sacred volume' or the 'religion of a book'. It has been all too possible for Christians so to use the Old Testament and the New Testament as a single corpus of inspired scripture as to interpret the latter in a kind of subservience to the former and even perversely to reverse their true relationship. It has been possible also to use the New Testament writings as a kind of uniform textbook, and to miss the creative dynamism of the history and the personalities which went to its making. Worst of all, it has been possible to see biblical revelation not as the witness of the writers to Jesus Christ but as a catena of things which 'the Bible says'. Thus the Bible says: Jesus is the Son of God; Jonah was three days and three nights in the belly of the whale; it is a shame for a man to have long hair; it is not permitted for a woman to speak in the assembly. It is not only that such literalism has again and again loomed large in the Church's use of the Bible. It is also that, even where literalism has been avoided, the idea that the Bible is a corpus of revelatory statements has been present if not in the consciousness at least in the subconsciousness of probably every Christian community through the centuries. Revelation is seen as the contents of a book rather than as the dynamic process of persons, events, and witness which brought the book into existence.

The last century saw the clash between the literalistic view of the Bible and the sciences of historical criticism and evolutionary biology. The convulsions which followed brought gains with which we are well familiar. Among these gains has been a renewed grasp of the dynamic history of revelation which preceded the formation of the biblical Canon. I want also to suggest that another gain, specially significant for our contemporary tasks, is a renewed understanding of the basic pattern of creation, fall, redemption, and union with Christ as the goal. The emergence of new insights can bring the recovery of old understandings.

1. The wonder and majesty of Creation may be no less apparent if it is seen not in the literal terms of the Genesis story but as a process through the evolution of nature with Man as the climax and the New Man in Christ as the eventual goal. Though

the apostolic writers never thought of creation in evolutionary terms and had no means of doing so, the descriptions of creation in relation to the eventual role of Christ in John 1, Romans 8, and Hebrews 2 can be read with new vividness as a result of our new knowledge of the evolutionary process.

2. As to the Fall, when we have ceased to think of it as something which Adam did in the garden of Eden we may more vividly see the Adam story as a superb parable of mankind's responsibility and mankind's deviation from it through pride, selfishness, and the stifling of conscience. With our experience of the modern history of civilization we may find Psalm 8 more than ever significant as a picture of Man's true role and Man's perversion of it. Psalm 8 gives a classic picture of Man possessing immense power over the world of nature while being himself under God's sovereignty. No evidence of Man's fallenness is more compelling than the story of Man within the present century when the vast increase of his powers has been so misused by fear, selfishness, and the self-aggrandizement of groups, nations, and races as to leave Man in impotence and frustration. We sin because we are part of a sinful situation and are bound to go on doing so, apart from divine grace bringing us into a new realm where death to self replaces self-seeking. In the light of new understanding of what it means to live in a fallen world we can enter with new sympathy into St Paul's language about the old Adam and the new man Christ, as well as his language about demonic powers. The depth and the range of our insight into the biblical drama may indeed be the greater without being wedded to an historical garden of Eden, for it is by no means clear from the Old Testament as a whole that Israel's own sense of sin and guilt was derived from, or dependent upon, the Adam and Eve story.

3. As to Revelation, it is a gain to be able to view this in terms of the historical process which preceded the formation of the two biblical Canons and a process which included a variety of literary media: drama, poetry, myth, symbol, as well as literal history and revelatory propositions. Indeed, the process of revelation may be the better understood if we do not shrink from considering not only the limitations of the human recipients of revelation in their cultural and historical setting but also

their ability to obscure what they were receiving by their limitations. May not the process of revelation in the scriptures be likened to a dialogue of disclosure and response? In his still valuable book, *Revelation and the Modern World*, Lionel Thornton, G.R., suggested that revelation consists of divine utterance and human response together, and the responses in part disclose and in part blur the divine action and word. By such a process the Truth of God is conveyed in the biblical writings; but when the story reaches the climax in Jesus Christ how different the relation of Word and response becomes. The divine Word now evokes the perfect response of perfect humanity in obedience, trust, love, worship, action. In Christ is the Yea, and in Christ also is the Amen. In Christ the Yea of revelation is unblurred and the Amen of response is flawless. Furthermore, Christ by his whole mission and his gift of the Holy Spirit enables men and women to be drawn into his response, and thus through him to know the truth and to grow up into the Christ-life which is Man's true goal.

In this way it appears that the scientific revolution in the study of the scriptures has not only illuminated the history which lies behind them but also given new vividness to the pattern of creation, fall, redemption by Jesus and redemption into Jesus as the goal: the pattern, or framework in which Jesus was first understood by the Christian Church.

In facing the problems involved in the presentation of Jesus Christ to the modern world, no undertaking has been more massive than that of Rudolf Bultmann. Combining a rare penetration into the meaning of the New Testament writings and a rare sensitivity to the contemporary world, Bultmann has set forward his thesis of demythologizing as the bridge between the two. His thesis has been that, by shedding the cosmological and philosophical framework within which the gospel was first preached and by conserving the existential challenge of the Cross as the essential gospel, we may find the gospel of Jesus Christ speaking with power in our contemporary world. I dare, however, to suggest that Bultmann's thesis is vitiated by two mistakes: a mistake concerning the needs of the modern world and a mistake concerning the apostolic age.

About the needs of the modern world, it seems arbitrary

to assume that existentialist philosophy has either such universal acceptance or such self-evident compulsion that it is our duty to preach Jesus in its terms alone. Indeed, in spite of the vogue of existentialist modes of thought there are minds which warm to a presentation of Jesus which relates him to creation and history; and there are hearts which are ready to respond to Jesus in a mystical context such as Protestantism has in the main disfavoured. If a man is not of the cast of mind and heart which Bultmann postulates, it may be that the demythologized Jesus will not speak to him, or if he does speak to him he may be rather different from the Jesus whom the apostles knew.

About the apostolic age, it is a mistake to suppose that the early Church did not attach importance or creative significance to the words and deeds of Jesus which belong to the period before the crucifixion. And is our knowledge of the history of Jesus before the crucifixion as minimal as is sometimes suggested? It may be impossible to find chronology or biography in the Gospel traditions, yet they may none the less yield us a credible picture of Jesus in relation to his contemporaries and of the way he saw his own role in relation to the coming of the kingdom of God, a role which contained within itself the seeds of Christology. I find it hard to doubt that both for the Christianity of the apostolic age and for the Christianity of today it matters not just that Christ died and rose again and confronts us with salvation, but that *this* Jesus, who was known as a person and is even now to some degree knowable, died and rose again and confronts us with a salvation which issues in a union with his own manhood.

It has been the theme of Bultmann that demythologizing can detach the gospel of Jesus Christ from the framework of Ptolemaic astronomy in which it was originally presented. It has been the contention of this lecture that the dual framework of primitive Christianity was not primarily the duality of Ptolemaic astronomy but the duality of Creator and creature. It is in relation to this duality of Creator and creature, rather than to any astronomical pattern, that the language of above, beyond, sending, coming, descending, breaking in, has its continuing place in Christian theology and liturgy. Attempts are sometimes made in contemporary theology to retain a divine Christ while extruding the duality in thought and the beyond element in language, and these attempts seem to issue in a kind of 'reductionism' and indeed to the suggestion that deity itself is an aspect of the created world.

It is indeed true that the 'beyond' element is very hard for minds formed by modern civilization to grasp, and indeed to many minds it is totally foreign and meaningless. But there has appeared within Western civilization a new hunger for the 'beyond' element which may prove to be very significant for Christianity as well as for religion in general. I am thinking of the awareness of the 'beyond' in those who pursue, or indeed grope after, mysticism in one or other of its forms. There are those who are finding in contemplation reality beyond the flux of the surface of life, reality which is no escapism as it enables the self to find its identity in a strenuous peace in touch with something which transcends.

While there is no necessary connection between Christianity and mysticism, it is not too much to say that mysticism involves that duality of God and the world, God and the self, in which the faith of the apostles may be understood. Unfortunately modern Christianity in the West has largely neglected its own mystical tradition in its concentration upon social activism and has thereby hindered its own presentation of its faith in a world in which mystical hunger is reviving.

It is therefore not irrelevant to the theme of this lecture to recall those Christian mystics who have at different times in history witnessed to the timeless factor in Christianity. In the year of her sexcentenary we may recall the Lady Julian of Norwich. Living in a time of catastrophe she saw in and through a vision of the Passion of Jesus a glimpse of the unity of creation, sin and pain, transfiguring grace, the goal of heaven—tied all together in the love of God which the Passion showed her. As Canon Allchin puts it: 'She sees in the Passion of Christ in which she participates all the suffering there ever was; the whole drama of man is summed up in one point. And when she speaks, she speaks as our contemporary.'

Julian's understanding of the oneness of the Christian pattern is rooted in her vivid vision of the Passion, when she desired like St Paul to know only Jesus Christ and him crucified. 'I conceived a mighty desire to receive these wounds in my life, the wound of very contrition, the wound of kind compassion, and the wound of steadfast longing towards God.' In the Passion she sees the black horror of sin; and in the same moment the horror of sin is pierced by the love of the Blessed Trinity, the love perfectly attained in the self-giving of Christ which caused him to suffer. In that love creation is held fast, and all existence is seen as a tiny hazel-nut in the hands of the Creator, and 'it lasteth and ever shall last for that God loveth it'. So, not apart from life's calamities but in the midst of them, there comes flooding in the vision of heaven whose essence is Christ himself, and the certainty that 'all shall be well and all manner of thing shall be well'.

No writer in the apostolic age wrote, and no Christian in the apostolic age describes this sort of experience, of the unity of truth in a single 'point': '*I saw God in a point*'. Biblically-minded theologians are apt to suppose that language of this kind is outside their concern. But in several passages in the New Testament there are flashes of insight into a pattern with the Passion of Jesus as the key: such flashes occur in Romans 8, in Hebrews 2, and in the Apocalypse. Julian is one of a number of mystics who in different periods of history have grasped in the vision of a single moment what is really the pattern of the apostolic faith: the good Creator, the sinful creature, sin and pain suffused by divine love, and Christ as himself the divine self-giving and himself the goal for Man. The point of coherence is Christ himself, whom to know is to be sure of the depth of Man's misery, the joy of God's heaven, and the hands of a faithful Creator.

The Last Beatitude

Thomas, because you have seen me, you believe. Happy are those who have not seen me and yet believe.   *John 20.29*

These words are the last of those sayings of our Lord recorded in the Gospels which we call the Beatitudes as they begin with the words 'happy, blessed, are those'. The first of the Beatitudes belong, as we all remember, to the Sermon on the Mount: happy are the poor in spirit, happy are the pure in heart, and the rest. Now, after the Resurrection, there comes the last Beatitude: happy are those who have not seen me and yet believe. Every one of us is included in this promise. None of us has seen our Lord, but all of us believe in him, for that is why we have come here to greet him on the day that commemorates his Resurrection.[1]

This is a day for joy, and not a day for argument. Yet I would recall the evidence upon which before even the Gospels were written the first Christians were convinced, and we too are convinced, that Jesus rose from the dead. On Friday evening the little group of friends took his body down from the Cross and buried it in a rock-hewn tomb nearby. His disciples were broken, his cause seemed to all to be defeated so as to rise no more. People no doubt were saying: 'Here is one more impostor, one more deluded man, given his due.' Yes, the disciples were broken. Now pass on a few weeks. These same disciples are boldly proclaiming to the nation that the Crucifixion was not a defeat and a disaster but itself the core of God's good news, because Jesus was alive and with them; and they were boldly summoning the nation to repent and believe. Something had happened—so as to bring about the great reversal and enable Christianity to exist. The disciples had their own explanation, which they gave at the time and went on giving throughout their lives. It was that Jesus had showed himself to them alive,

[1] Sermon preached in Canterbury Cathedral, Easter 1972.

not once only but a number of times, with his own convincing
personal impression upon them. Was this true? or was it a
delusion? Here I am struck by a point which impresses me as
specially convincing. So far from their Easter experiences being
cosily comforting and suiting their own assumptions, the disciples
found their Easter experiences revealing to them new truths,
new calls to adventure and self-sacrifice, new challenges to
their minds and actions. Did all this come from their own fancy,
or was it true that Jesus, alive, was making himself known to
them? It is the former theory which seems to me to strain
credibility, and rejecting it I join with the Church down the ages
in its joyful cry, 'the Lord is risen, he is risen indeed'.

It is from St John's account that our text comes. By the
evening of Easter Day besides the women who had visited the
tomb there were ten apostles who knew the secret: only ten
of the company which had been called the Twelve. Judas had
left the Upper Room on Thursday night to go on his traitor's
errand. Another was absent now: Thomas, who had been ready
to die with Jesus and had said, 'Let us also go that we may die
with him', Thomas who had at the Supper asked Jesus about
the way he was going. The evangelist tells us that Thomas was
not with the others on the first Easter evening; he missed the
first of the Easter appearances. He had not seen the Lord, and
when he heard the story he was sceptical. Was it really true, or
was it fantasy? He brooded. He hesitated. His eyes must see,
his hands must touch the wounds of Jesus.

A week later, on the day we call Low Sunday, the chance
comes. Jesus is with them. And Thomas is with them too.
Jesus offers the doubter all that he asked for, and more. Thomas,
come and see, come and touch. And Thomas will not wait to
accept what the Lord offers him; his heart, his mind, and his
voice leap ahead, ahead of any declaration of faith that any of
the disciples had made: My Lord and My God. And the answer
of Jesus reaches beyond Thomas to all of us: Thomas saw and
believed, all of us are happy because without having ever seen
we believe all the same.

So to all of us the last Beatitude is spoken. Happy are you,
you in any century, you in any place, you in Canterbury in 1972,
you in any part of the world, you perhaps who are in cruel
grief and sorrow, you perhaps who are bewildered and frustrated:

happy are you, happy because though you do not see Jesus your Easter faith is sure.

What is this faith which we can possess? It is unlike the faith of Thomas, for it is not based upon touch or sight. Yet it is like the faith of Thomas, it must always be like the faith of Thomas, in two significant ways.

First, an Easter faith which is true is always a faith which includes the wounds of Calvary. When Christ was raised from the dead, it did not mean that the Cross was left behind. Far from it, the risen Christ is always the Christ who was once crucified. Cross and Resurrection go together. Christian imagery and Christian art have portrayed this through the centuries. We recall pictures of the Crucifixion which show the kingly triumph, the majestic peace already breaking through the scene of death. We recall pictures of the risen Jesus which show the marks of sacrifice never effaced and carried into the risen glory. And the art and the imagery convey deep truth. We can never know the risen Jesus and never serve him unless we face the reality of the Cross. We must still repent of the sins which wound him, as our sins always do. We must still find him in those who suffer as we go and serve him in them. Never can the notes of Calvary fade from the Church's songs of victory.

Do you remember the story of St Martin and his vision? One day Martin, the soldier-saint, was praying, and there appeared before him a blazing light and within it was a radiant, joyful figure, robed like a king with a jewelled crown and gold-embroidered shoes. And his voice said: 'Martin, recognize him whom you see. I am Christ. I am about to descend to the earth, and I am showing myself to you first.' A moment or two later the voice went on: 'Why do you hesitate, Martin, to believe me? I am Christ.' And Martin replied: 'The Lord Jesus did not foretell that he would come in purple and crowned in gold. I will not believe that Christ is come unless I see him in the dress and in the form in which he suffered.' The apparition vanished. Martin knew it was a temptation of the devil. There is the issue. If the Easter faith is to prevail in the world it will not be through a 'triumphalist' Church, but a Church which has the marks of sacrifice.

The second way in which our faith must resemble that of St Thomas is that it must be a faith which says, My Lord and My

God. What a declaration that was! Now what are we saying when as Christians we declare, My Lord and My God? *My God:* here is the great doctrine that Jesus is divine and without idolatry we may worship him, God of God, light of light, true God of true God. *My Lord:* here is an act of moral allegiance and obedience, the commitment of ourselves to a master and to a way of life. Thomas had said in an earlier episode, 'Let us also go that we may die with him', and at the Last Supper he had said, 'How can we know the way?' If we own Jesus as Lord we are setting ourselves to a practical allegiance which again and again will be asking, 'What am I to *do* about this or that problem?' and 'Is Jesus the Lord of my attitudes, my prejudices, my human relationships?' My Lord and My God, the ethics and the doctrine go together.

Happy, then, are those who have not seen and yet have faith. Ours is a faith *unlike* that of Thomas in that our eyes have never seen Jesus and while we have our own experience of him our acceptance of the history rests upon the witness of the apostles. But let ours be a faith *like* that of Thomas, a faith which faces the wounds of Jesus and a faith which is never separated from practical obedience. And such a faith receives not only the blessing spoken in the hearing of Thomas, 'Happy are those who have not seen and yet believe', but the earlier blessing spoken on the mount in Galilee, 'Happy are the pure in heart, for they shall see God.'

The Historical Jesus and the Christian Faith

I find on the fly-leaf of my copy of Charles Gore's *Belief in God* the words scribbled: 'Michael Ramsey, October 1923'. I was then a freshman at Cambridge within a few weeks of matriculation, not yet twenty years old, and studying the classics; and this must have been the first book of a theological kind that I ever bought or read. The impression of the book upon me went deep and remained through the years; and even now when I pose a theological question to myself I often ask myself, perhaps half-consciously, where I am agreeing or disagreeing with Charles Gore. So you will understand that a certain reminiscent emotion is with me tonight[1] when having reached the age which Gore was when he wrote *Belief in God* after his retirement from the see of Oxford I discuss with you the question of Christian faith and the historical Jesus of which he made me aware almost half a century ago.

There were other works of Gore which dealt more fully with the historical Jesus, and others which dealt more profoundly with the meaning of faith. But it is in *Belief in God* that he shows most characteristically his view of Christianity as a religion which stands or falls by the credibility of the historical records of Jesus of Nazareth. I recall the course of his thesis. First, he invokes the traditional arguments, and especially the argument from experience, as pointers to ethical theism. Then he asks whether the God whom conscience has tentatively affirmed will not make himself known in particular actions; and we pass quickly to the Hebrew prophets from Amos to Jesus Christ upon whom Gore sets immense weight as a phenomenon inexplicable apart from their own explanation: 'Thus saith the Lord.' The content of the prophetic faith in God is then put to the test of reason and is found to be compatible with our knowledge of the nature of the world. Yet, the moral disorder of the world being what it

[1] The Gore lecture delivered in Westminster Abbey, 16 November 1971.

is, the faith in the God of righteousness and love breaks down
unless God acts decisively to deal with the world's disorder.
So we come to the history of Jesus. Is that history credible?
Here Gore claims to write solely as an objective historical critic,
applying the methods of historical science. And, in brief, his answer
is: yes, the historical records about Jesus are credible because
Mark was an accurate recorder of Peter's simple and straight-
forward memories, and Luke was a good historian able to use
his sources competently. Therefore the history of Jesus is secure,
unless in concert with many misguided modern critics you have
an *a priori* prejudice against the credibility of miracle. Space
is then given to the exposure of that prejudice; and indeed it is
in expounding the significance of miracle that Gore does some
of his finest writing. By miracle God asserts the divine freedom
which can be no less than the human freedom which has distorted
the world on a massive scale; and by miracle God asserts the
law of his righteous purpose amidst the lawlessness of sin.
Gore speaks of 'the assurance given by Christ's resurrection from
the dead that at the last issue the power which rules in the physical
world is on the side of righteousness, that it is the same God
as commands in conscience and speaks through prophets'.
William Temple was at first shocked, but in later life came to
appreciate an outburst of Gore, perhaps only half serious: 'Were
it not for the resurrection I would see no more reason for believing
that God was revealed in Jesus than that he was revealed in
the Emperor Nero.'

It was the deeply moral strain in Gore's discussion, the will
to set the historical questions in the context of the righteousness
of the God of the prophets, together with an agonizingly visible
integrity, which won him ardent disciples and made it seem
audacious to differ from him. Yet the closely-knit coherence of
his position brought its own difficulties. Suppose that historians
reach other conclusions about the birth or the life or the resurrection of Jesus, or even introduce a few thin ends of sceptical
wedges into the history, then the fabric of faith begins to shake.
Hence the vehemence with which Gore would defend every
inch of the historical ground, sure all the time of the scientific
validity of his own criticism. Hence too the touchiness about
any shifting of the line between what is history and what is
symbol in the Creed. Before he died in 1932 not a few of his

disciples had become aware of the criticism which Hoskyns voices in a letter to Albert Mansbridge:

> Gore was one of the pioneers in accepting the critical approach to the study of the Bible. Later on he seemed to have allowed the right of the critic up to a certain point, after which Gore became rigid and was apt to be harsh. Personally I think this was not because he really refused to see what his own critical principles involved, but because he genuinely thought certain views were sound and others cranky and critically doubtful. But whatever the cause, at the end Gore did draw a line through the critical movement, which meant that he ceased to be a leader in Biblical exegesis.[1]

How vastly has the scene of the historical study of Jesus of Nazareth changed. It is to this altered scene that I devote the rest of this lecture. Perhaps the first startling symbol of the change was the publication of R. H. Lightfoot's Bampton Lectures of 1934, two years after Gore's death, with the title *History and Interpretation in the Gospels. Formgeschichte*, which had been familiar on the continent of Europe before the 1920s began and had been introduced to the American continent with indeed an acute counter-criticism by B. S. Easton in 1929, was strangely neglected in England even by a scholar as familiar with Germany as Hoskyns. But with R. H. Lightfoot the new method came on to the English campus, and came to stay. The new method disallows the idea that the Gospels give us diary-memoirs or biographies; it disallows the distinction, made not only by Gore but by a host of New Testament scholars of the time, between factual history and interpretation. It sees the Gospels as the outcome of a long process of oral tradition in the Christian communities, a tradition inevitably shaped by the theology, the piety, the didactic and apologetic needs of the post-resurrection Church. Inevitably the methods of form-criticism have posed in a new way the question: Do the Gospels give us a picture of what Jesus actually did and taught? or have we no more than a whisper of his voice and a tracing of the outskirts of his ways?

[1] Quoted in J. Carpenter, *Gore, A Study in Liberal Catholic Thought* (London 1960), p. 104.

How then may we approach the history of Jesus? Let us start with three facts which no reputable historian will want to deny. Jesus existed. Jesus died by crucifixion. Subsequently the phenomenon of Christianity came about. Now history has to explain not only how Christianity came about after the crucifixion of Jesus, but also one remarkable characteristic of it from the start. It included a new valuation of suffering and death as being not the marks of defeat and disaster but as things positive and creative. This is seen in the teachings, the liturgies, the ethics, the way of life, the practical behaviour of the Christians; and it is bound up with a conviction about the crucifixion of Jesus. This horrible event is not ignominy, defeat, disgrace: it is good news, a divine action which has brought salvation.

How did this conviction, integral as it was to the phenomenon of Christianity in history, come about? It is true that according to the traditions within the Synoptic Gospels Jesus gave to the disciples teaching about the significance of his death. But it is clear that up to the time of the crucifixion they had not grasped this teaching or absorbed it. When Jesus died, the secret died with him. Something happened, not only to cause the Church to recover and survive but also to cause the astonishing assurance that the death of Jesus was good news. Something happened. The apostles said that what had happened was that Jesus made himself known to them as alive: seeing, hearing, and receiving the impact of his person upon them, as he gave them not comforting illusions but challenges to new actions and new understandings. Either the apostles were deluded in their conviction that Jesus was with them again, and their subsequent life and behaviour were rooted in delusion, or else it was really true that Jesus had risen.

Like Gore I find the evidence for the resurrection compelling historically. Unlike him I put the emphasis less upon the particular traditions about the mode of the resurrection and more upon the total experience of the apostles. And within the evidence I see a considerable factor in the apostles' conviction that the Cross is now good news. It seems very significant in the apostles' understanding of the resurrection that it is the return to them of the Jesus who died, the Jesus to whom the wounds still belong. Thus to believe in Jesus as risen Lord meant and still means to pledge oneself to the Cross. Therefore I find myself near to

Bultmann in seeing the Easter faith as an act of commitment to the death of Jesus. But I part company with Bultmann in being convinced that the resurrection was an event; and while various factors enter into my belief in it, it was an event to which the historic evidence is relevant as showing that without the resurrection the course of known history is unaccountable.

What now of the life of Jesus which preceded the crucifixion?

Much is made in contemporary studies of the contention that the Gospels give us not diaries or photographs or simple memoirs but interpretative portraits. So be it. But if the interpretations are true interpretations, then the portraits may be of real historical value. The crucial question is whether the Christian communities created the figure of Jesus whom they portrayed, or whether they were themselves created by a figure of Jesus whose elusive originality their portraiture has not concealed. Need we regret it if our knowledge of Jesus is through the media of interpretations of him within the growing understanding of the early Church? One of the attractive recent theses of a conservative kind is that of the Swedish scholar, Harald Riesenfeld, who would persuade us that much of the tradition about Jesus was handed down from the start by a process of dictation and memorizing in the manner of the rabbis. But if this were so, would we really be gainers? I quote some words of the Jesuit scholar Xavier Léon-Dufour in his book *Les Évangiles et l'Histoire de Jésus*: 'If the early Church had issued only one authorised and authoritative life of Jesus, the rationalist historian would probably never have realised what Jesus meant to his followers.'[1] Again: 'The disciples were concerned not only with remembering the teaching of Jesus, like the pupils of a rabbi, but with understanding and applying the spirit of his teaching.'[2]

On the other hand, there are some striking ways in which the synoptic tradition seems to show a pre-crucifixion perspective. Certain of the great themes of post-resurrection Christianity are not read back into the tradition, and appear only in a few anticipatory hints in the sayings of Jesus. Examples are the theme of the dominance of the Holy Spirit and the theme of the universality of the gospel as being for all nations. No more than

---

[1] E.T., *The Gospels and the Jesus of History*, p. 192.
[2] Ibid., p. 199.

a few hints of these great themes are present; and we see in the tradition the sowing of the seeds of the doctrine by Jesus rather than the full fruition which the Church came to know.

Unable as we therefore are to search in the Gospels for biography or for diary memoirs, we are none the less able by scientific procedure to gain a picture of Jesus in relation to his contemporaries. We ask what are the themes about Jesus which are well attested within a number of strands in the tradition, in sayings, in parables, in episodes. Asking that, we get a picture of Jesus in his various relationships with the scene around him. Thus, Jesus is one who searches for the outcasts in society and befriends them. Jesus is lonely, cut off from home and family as he pursues his mission. Jesus is vividly conscious of the presence, sovereignty, and graciousness of God in nature and in the lives of men and women. Jesus shows that a new order is here, breaking in, an order which fulfils the scriptures. Jesus predicts judgement upon the Jewish church. Jesus trains disciples to be the nucleus of a new Israel with whom a new covenant is made. Jesus accepts death as his vocation, and he foresees beyond his death a divine victory depicted in a variety of images. By this procedure we gain a picture of Jesus in relation to his contemporaries in Palestine.

Let us look more closely at the central theme, the kingdom of God, and then at the claim of Jesus in relation to it.

Jesus preaches: 'The time is fulfilled, the kingdom of God has arrived, repent, and believe the good news' (Mark 1.14). He presents this theme by mighty works and by the teaching of the divine righteousness. That Jesus did perform mighty works is clear not only from episodes describing them but from sayings and controversies about them, including the allegation that he did them by the prince of the devils. But as to Jesus's presentation of the kingdom and its righteousness, we miss its intensity and its originality if we concentrate solely upon passages which describe 'the kingdom' as such in parables or otherwise. It is not only that Jesus says this or that about the kingdom; it is that he witnesses with a rare vividness to the nearness and sovereignty of God, in nature and in everyday human situations. God is near, God is here, in sovereignty, in generosity, in piercing challenge. Responding to God's providence men will be trustful and not anxious. Responding to his generosity they will be loving and forgiving to one another. Responding to his sovereignty they will renounce power, importance, claims for themselves. The rich man can no more enter the kingdom of God than a camel can crawl through the tiny eye of a needle. Why? Because he is too big, he has power, importance in himself and his possessions. Those who approach like children are not too big, the kingdom is for them.

It is in this context that we see the cleavage between Jesus and the contemporary religion of the law. Where did the cleavage lie? It was not that Jesus was attacking the law. On one occasion at least, the Corban controversy, he upheld the law of honour to father and mother against a tradition which sought to evade it. Nor would it have been remarkable or necessarily a cause of resentment for Jesus to support liberal interpretations of the law; there were Pharisees who did this, not least those of the school of Hillel. No, Jesus was demanding an obedience to the law far more radical than its official teachers understood: an obedience going to the roots of motive as well as to outward action and involving positive acts of goodness as well as the negative avoidance of certain evils. This meant that Jesus was bringing men and women into touch not just with the law but with the God whose law it is, the God whose holiness requires total obedience to him and whose compassion requires total compassion to others on any day of the week. It was a message about God and God's sovereignty. It therefore cut at the heart of the idea that just to keep the law is the way to spiritual security. There is no spiritual security. It is idle for the rich young ruler to say: 'All this I have observed from my youth up.' It is idle for the Pharisee in the parable to count upon fasting twice in the week and giving tithes of all he possessed, for righteousness is about God and about humility. The law cannot save, God whose law it is can save and does.

The kingdom is, however, coming not as a general proposition but as a specific event. Sayings and parables show this. Something is happening. Decision is urgent. There can be no dallying. Here is the harvest. Reap it. Here is a precious pearl. Buy it at once. Here is a door. Hurry through it. And all this because 'the time' is here, the old order is breaking up, the new order is come. 'Blessed are the eyes which see what you see. For, I tell you, many prophets and kings desired to see what you see, and did not see it, and to hear what you hear, and did not hear it' (Luke 10.23; cf. Matt. 13.17). It is within this vision of fulfilment that the role of Jesus himself is seen.

It is concerning the claims made by Jesus that the contrast is considerable between the outlook of the older scholarship and the outlook common today where form-critical methods are used. It is a frequent contention of contemporary scholars that the titles used in recorded sayings of Jesus, Son, Son of God, Son of Man, Lord, do not belong to primitive tradition but were read into the tradition in the light of post-resurrection Christology. Some scholars would except from this formula the title Son of Man, allowing that it may have been used by Jesus of himself in mysterious reference to his suffering and his glory. But I would contend that not nearly so much turns upon this question as we might at first sight suppose. On any showing Jesus avoided identifying himself with current messianic conceptions, and if he acknowledged Messiahship at the time of Peter's confession, at his entrance into Jerusalem on Palm Sunday, and in his response to Caiaphas at the trial, it was Messiahship with an immense difference. Whatever messianic role Jesus had he linked with a mission ending in suffering and death as his vocation. It seems to me that both for history and for Christology the significant thing is not a list of the titles Jesus used, or might have used, but the nature of the authority with which he spoke and the implied claims about his role in relation to mankind.

The claims are seen in the context of Jesus's own self-effacement. His message is not about himself. He is absorbed in the sovereignty, the purpose, and the presence of God. Yet the implied claims recur. It is Jesus who will accept or reject men in the future judgement (Matt. 7.21–2). It is for Jesus that the renunciations of discipleship are made (Mark 8.37). It is Jesus's death that will bring deliverance (Mark 10.45) and be the ground of a new covenant (Mark 14.24). His authority was quite unlike that of the rabbis. It was an authority which caused the crowd to disperse on the day when the five thousand men—perhaps bent upon a messianic rising—were fed, an authority which cleared the temple at a word, an authority which led the Roman centurion to see in Jesus a power over events akin to his own power over his soldiers. 'Come unto me'; 'He that loves father and mother more than me is not worthy of me'; 'Follow me, and let the dead bury their own dead.' It is interesting to notice that the treatment of this implied authority by C. H. Dodd in a few pages of his recent book, *The Founder of Christianity*, is very similar to the treatment of it by Gore in a few pages in his *Belief in Christ*. Was Gore's summing-up unscientific or unjust: 'The implication of authority which seems to inhere in the words and tone of Jesus does seem to me to express, if not the jealousy of God, then some sort of quality as lies at the heart of all spiritual tyranny and false sacerdotalism.'?[1]

The mission of Jesus both struck at the religious security of Judaism and avoided involvement in political Messianism. It led to such resentment by both the Pharisees and the party of the high priests that they plotted to destroy him. Of this there is no historical doubt. Nor can there reasonably be doubt that Jesus saw his coming death as lying within the divine purpose as part of his mission. If form-criticism warns us against putting weight upon the formal and systematized predictions of the death and the resurrection, there remain sayings which show the will of Jesus to accept the death, his linking of it with a new covenant, and the frustration which he feels until it happens. 'I have a baptism to be baptized with and how am I constrained until it is accomplished' (Luke 12.50). With the covenant there is the new *ecclesia*. The disciples were trained to be its nucleus, and within it the apostles would be rulers. But their rule would be rooted in a humility like that of Jesus who is among them as he who serves. When Jesus died, however, they all were scattered. It seemed the end for Jesus, and the end for the *ecclesia*. Then something happened.

Such is the picture of the mission of Jesus which the Gospel traditions provide as credible history. The picture seems to make sense in relation to its environment, while its originality makes it hard to think it could be the product of that environment. It seems also that the inevitable reading-in of post-resurrection interpretation does not obliterate the traces of a primitive perspective. Above all, it seems that the traditions, belonging as they do to the Church's preaching and teaching, bear the impress not only of a theology but of a person, a person in whom authority and self-effacement were strangely blended. While

[1] *The Reconstruction of Belief* (London 1926), p. 349.

it seems that the mission of Jesus was a puzzle until the death and the resurrection unfolded its meaning, it is hard to see how the resurrection could of itself have created Christianity without the sowing of seeds in the previous words and actions of Jesus. It was the impressions of the whole, the person, the teaching, the death, the resurrection, which led the apostles to the conclusion that Jesus is no less than Lord, Son of God, the image of invisible deity, the Word who was in the beginning.

How big are the differences between the critical procedures which I have been trying to use and those of Charles Gore and others of his time?

First, Gore, like many both of his allies and his antagonists at the time, thought that to get at history you need to distinguish it sharply from interpretation. First get the story, then build the interpretation upon it. But the Gospels were not written like that. History and interpretative preaching were from the first days of the Church intermingled. Yet if my thesis tonight is valid, it is possible to be sure that the Gospels came from such a milieu and none the less to claim that we know reliable facts about the story of Jesus.

Second, Gore thought that given the absence of subversive presuppositions the facts could be ascertained and believed on strictly evidential procedure, and then the theology could be derived almost compulsively from the facts. It is not as simple as that. I would say that my own belief in the resurrection includes indeed the strictly evidential consideration that without the resurrection other history becomes incredible; but it also includes a certain attitude to the biblical theism and a certain response to the claims and impression of Jesus. Faith can find confirmation in a rigorous appeal to history, but can that appeal to history of itself create faith?

Third, what of the supernatural? If the apostles' estimate of Jesus is true, then the whole action of his birth, death, and rising again may fairly be called supernatural as being a unique disclosure of God in history and in humanity. Because this is so it seems to me that two things follow. One is that it would not be surprising if incidents of a non-normal kind occurred, and the historian can weigh the evidence in each case without prejudice. The other is that it would not be surprising if the tradition also included symbolic language as a mode of expressing the belief that the mission of Jesus was divine as well as human. Gore would never allow this possibility, but in his vehement refusal to allow it he may have been missing the variety of factors within the traditions and also missing the point that it is the divine character of the mission of Jesus which makes credible both miracle and the presence of symbolic writing. For myself I have come through the years to think that while miracle occurred the supernatural is perhaps most significantly seen less in miracle as such than in the divine self-giving in the death and the resurrection together. Does not the Fourth Gospel suggest that while the glory was apparent in the signs wrought by Jesus the glory was most signally apparent in the death on Calvary?

But it is time for me to stop. How great have been the changes in scientific method and in the modes of theological approach since the day when I carried home my copy of Gore's *Belief in God* and began a lifetime's study of the historical Jesus and the Christian faith. But after all the changes we still know a good deal about the history of Jesus of Nazareth; and what we know evokes from me, at least, the response: My Lord and my God.

The Message of F. D. Maurice

The true light that lighteth every man was coming into the world.

John 1.9

We are met here[1] to commemorate a great Christian, Frederick Denison Maurice, and in thanking God for him many of us will have thoughts of gratitude for those who aroused our awareness of him in times when he was forgotten. In this I cannot be alone in feeling a debt to J. O. F. Murray, the former Master of Selwyn, whose devotion to Maurice was scarcely less than his devotion to Hort. Murray took a leading part in causing the commemorative tablet to be placed in this church where Maurice ended his ministry.

Cambridge knew 'F.D.M.' as one who for all the tempestuousness of his character could bring serenity and peace to other people. Julia Wedgwood recalls this quaint story of his earlier Cambridge period.

> Five Cambridge men were talking over a recent execution, previous to which the Chaplain of the gaol had spent the whole day with the condemned man; and all agreed that there were very few persons whose presence at such a time would not add a new horror to death. The conversation then turned on the choice which each would make, in the last hours of life, of a companion to accompany him to its utmost verge; and it was agreed by all five that each should write down the name of the person he would choose; and the papers when opened were found to contain a single name—Maurice.[2]

Throughout his life there were those who were grateful for his gift of bringing calm, peace, security in God, while in himself

---

[1] In the Church of St Edward the King, Cambridge, 23 March 1972, at a service for the centenary of Maurice's death.

[2] Julia Wedgwood, *Twentieth-Century Teachers* (1900), p. 29.

he often seemed a man tormented: 'all twisted, screwed, wire-drawn', as Carlyle once said of him. But in the last phase, here in St Edward's, his friends rejoiced to find him visibly showing in himself the peace he had so often distributed to others. An observer wrote: 'The rush of his start for a walk had now gone. His movements, like his life, became quiet and measured—there was a beauty which seemed to shine round him. . . . It made undergraduates not specially impressionable stop and watch him.'

A price had been paid for this serenity. Maurice was not one of those who on one level live tumultuously and on another level enjoy an inner calm, like an ocean stormy on the surface and tranquil in its depths below. No, the peace he sought, the peace he strove for, was always God's peace snatched out of storms and conflicts which were God's storms and conflicts. It fell to him to grasp hold of God, or rather to find God grasping hold of him, amidst many battles he was fighting. To Maurice every one of his conflicts was a conflict about God. Thus: against Pusey, what sort of God is it whose baptism is the gate of an exclusive salvation and not a sign of the redemption of the whole human family? Against the Evangelicals, what sort of God is it whose anger needs appeasing by the satisfaction of a Son's death? Against the liberals, what sort of God is it who can be equated with human ideas about his reasonableness? Against Colenso, what sort of God is it to whom history is a branch of arithmetic? Against Mansel, what sort of God is it whom not to know is eternal life? It was God who made him a man of conflict: 'Thou art stronger than I, and thou hast prevailed.' Often there were foes in front and foes behind at once. Hear him, for instance, speaking about the Working Men's College:

> I have felt that a Working College, if it is to do something, must be in direct hostility to the secularists. . . . But to do this effectively it must also be in direct hostility to the religionists, that is to say it must assert the principle that God is sought and honoured in every pursuit and not merely in something technically called religion.

Maurice's conflicts were filled again and again with exasperations about language. There were those who warmed to his use of words and found them conveying God and Christ to them in a way which helped them greatly. There were those, certainly more numerous among the theologians, whom his use of words could drive into frenzies of exasperation. There were those who nearly understood, but before long found themselves in a mist. Now partly it was that Maurice was a bad writer, as was only too likely in one for whom writing and talking and poking the fire were dangerously mixed up. Yet while clarity of words wedded to clarity of mind can be used by God's servants to grasp and expound his truth, the same clarity can also distort and deceive by being more neat than God ever can be. I believe it was sometimes the sense of this divine quarrel with language which helped to make Maurice obscure, and sometimes in his obscurity he could be telling truth which clearer words might utterly fail to tell. The Regius Professor of Modern History writes of him: 'He felt the heart of God flaming, and knew it as indescribable in human language. Words tormented him because they could hardly unveil truth, yet truth must be unveiled, and by words.' There lay at once his strength and his weakness.

In the century since Maurice's death one who was widely known as the man of strife has increasingly been discovered as saying things which belong to our peace. I recall some of the ways in which this has happened, ways for which Christians have come to be grateful, though at different periods and never always in quite the same way.

The contrast between God and religion was thundered forth by Karl Barth in the years between the wars and since. But for our English scene perhaps no one has done more to illuminate the contrast than Maurice. 'We have been dosing our people with religion, when what they want is not that but the living God.'

The sense that creeds and formulas are not themselves truth but witnesses to the actions of God in Christ who is the truth has had many exponents. But who did more than Maurice, after he returned to us, to bring this home amidst the complacency of our English orthodoxy?

The method whereby you look first to the truth which lurks within the erroneous positions you are trying to combat is a method as necessary for any civilized discussion as it is for sound theology. But how often is it tragically lacking. Has the method ever had a more wide-ranging illustration than in Maurice's *The Kingdom of Christ: Letters to a Quaker*? If this is perhaps one of the few matters about which we do rather better than the Victorians, our debt to Maurice is considerable.

Then there is Maurice's power of relating the theme of Christ's redemption in gospel and Church to the created order of the world. He shows this power not just in synthetic statement of doctrine, such as a good many theologians have made, but in a kind of sensitivity to the human scene which peeps out again and again in his pages. The Bible, the Gospel, the Incarnation, are about not only people as they are meant to become but people just as they are.

Lastly, linked with the previous theme, is the lesson that beneath the perversions of sin and cruelty there is within the created world a shape, a shape reflecting the Triune God who made it. To bring the world to Christ is to uncover what the world really is. Dig and go on digging, for the foundation is there to find.

All this is familiar 'Mauriciana'. To some of us parts of the debt mean more than others. There is the churchman who learns from Maurice that the 'Signs of the Constitution of the Catholic Church of Christ' are signs not of an exclusive system but of an inclusive divine gift. And there is the social reformer who learns the big difference between uncovering a divine order for society and trusting to a theory of progress without God. In every case the debt to the ideas is mingled with the debt to the man, for every idea was hammered out on the anvil of his own human conflicts. Never can there have been a teacher whose teaching was more costly to himself. He lived it all, and he suffered it all.

If, however, you ask me what I think Maurice can with most singular advantage show us today, I would name a theme which could exasperate as much as any and yet may show part of the secret.

Julia Wedgwood recalls: 'Some readers will remember the bedridden woman who was always being introduced to us as the infallible arbiter of spiritual problems perplexing to the minds of scholars and profound thinkers, generally in order to rebuke the pride of our intellect but nearly as often that she might reflect upon our spiritual exclusiveness.' In a rather similar vein J. B. Mozley wrote of one of Maurice's theories which he was criticizing: 'We know he will maintain the urgent necessity of preaching the great practical truth to peasants and labourers, to ploughmen and villagers, in fields and market places, that he is convinced that these masses of uninformed minds are crying out for this especial truth and are hungry and desperate for it.'[1]

These strictures had some justice. Maurice was liable in a rather maddening way to try to turn a corner in an intellectual argument by an abrupt appeal to the view of the common man or woman: 'any housewife knows', 'any patient in a hospital can tell you'. Yet the strictures touched only half of the case. Maurice knew better than many of his contemporaries that Christian truth is about every man and woman and child. Theology is about them, or it is not about God at all. It is not that the untrained prejudices of everyman can be the arbiter of a theological problem, and when Maurice sometimes spoke as if that were so he was caricaturing his own position. No, theology is about every man. In the old words of St Irenaeus: 'the vision of God is the glory of man'.

The Church has always professed to know this but has not always shown that she knows it with Maurice's shocking simplicity. If today there is a more vivid awareness that theology in being about God is also about every man and woman and child, then Maurice is rejoicing. Never was this aspect of his theology and of himself, an aspect which he did himself sometimes caricature, more visible than in his last ministry here at St Edward's. The people saw, and they remembered specially his way with the children when he taught them in the catechism and his way with the sick when he visited them.

It was on 1 April 1872, Easter Monday, that Maurice died. In his last days of great weakness there was that rare mingling of care for theology and care for people. On Easter Eve he dictated a letter resigning St Edward's and signing his name for the last time. Through his illness he had spoken at intervals about his sense of not having previously known what it was that the sick wanted, and of feeling that if he were to recover he would know better how to help them. After deciding with

[1] J. B. Mozley, *Essays Historical and Theological*, II, p. 299.

a great struggle to resign St Edward's he said to his wife: 'If I may not have St Edward's at least I may hope to give myself more to the work of the hospital.'

The revised lectionary had just been published. He said he thought the restoring of the Book of Revelation to the regular lessons was the greatest boon that had been given to the Church for a long time. 'People talk of the poor not being able to understand the Book of Revelation. It is just the poor who do take it in.'

He was constantly speaking with horror of the divisions of the Church, and when it was reported to him that some new prosecution was threatened he became so agitated that he could only be quieted by being told it was only a rumour and not authenticated.

Easter Day came. They read to him the Emmaus story. He looked out of the window. 'All those people,' he said, 'who are walking about there, with their doubts and thoughts, whether frivolous thoughts or earnest doubts, whatever they may be, need a Friend to give himself to them and to bring them out; not to quench the doubts as I too often have done.'

On Easter night he grew weaker. The next morning the Holy Communion was to be brought to him. But no.

He began talking very rapidly, but very indistinctly. We made out that it was about the Communion being for all nations and peoples, for men who were working like Dr Radcliffe (his physician). Something too about it being the work of women to teach to men its meaning. . . . He went on speaking, but more and more indistinctly, till suddenly he made a great effort, and after a pause he said slowly and distinctly: 'The knowledge of the love of God, the blessing of God Almighty, the Father, the Son and the Holy Ghost, be amongst you, amongst us, and remain for ever.'

Seldom can a man's last hours have so gathered in one his work and himself. They thanked God for him, and so a hundred years later do we.

Christ and Humanism[1]

Christianity and Humanism stand today in contrast as rival concepts. It was not always so. Europe knew a long tradition of avowedly Christian humanism drawn from the confluence of the stream of biblical theism from Palestine and the stream of classical humanism from ancient Greece. But humanism has come to mean a reverence for man and a concern for his dignity, morality, and happiness linked with a belief that these ends are best served by the advance of the scientific outlook and by the demise of religion, since religion thwarts the scientific outlook and distracts man from his effectiveness in this world by an irrelevant preoccupation with another.

Though the modern form of the debate is new it has many echoes of the past. To the Jew of the Bible man was a frail being, a creature of the God who made him, and while he posses-sed dignity and power within the world these were his because the Creator bestowed them and they were enjoyed in a spirit of humble dependence. The psalmist's words, 'I thank thee, O God, for I am fearfully and wonderfully created', expressed, and still express, the biblical view of man. To the Greeks of the ages of their greatest poetry man's dignity was autonomous. The line of Sophocles, 'Many things are marvellous and nothing is more marvellous than man', is matched by the Athenian sculptors in their tracing of the beauty of the human body. True, the Greeks knew man to be fearful in the presence of Fate and cautious in the presence of deities who might be jealous of him; but his dignity was not derived from the deities who were often his moral inferiors.

Echoes of those ancient contrasts are not absent from the very modern volume before us. In *The Humanist Outlook*, edited by A. J. Ayer,[2] twenty essayists put us in their debt by a very comprehensive account of humanist ideals and methods. The essays give a picture of the claims made for scientific method,

[1] This essay is reproduced by permission of the *Spectator*.
[2] London, Pemberton, 1968.

of morals as the humanist sees them, of some specific human problems as a humanist attacks them, of the humanist critique of Christianity, and of the hopes for humanity which it is possible to cherish. One historical piece is included, a sketch of the Cambridge Heretics 1909 to 1932, in which Sargant Florence delightfully recalls some Cambridge figures of the time.

What picture emerges? Despite some contradictions amongst the essays a distinct approach to human life becomes clear. Humanism is not an unbounded regard for the power of reason, but a confidence that the use of scientific method can do humanity more good than anything else can. Where religion and scientific method try to assist man in his problems the latter can do well what the former does badly. Though humanist ethics are sometimes not at variance with the ethics of religion, the ground of humanist ethics is always different—not 'what God wills' but 'what is good for man'. But not seldom the content of the two types of morals differs, and it is claimed that Christian ethics are 'supernatural' and tinged with an anti-social ascetic otherworldliness whereas humanist ethics are 'social' and directed to man's fulfilment in the human community. But meanwhile it is acknowledged that humanism needs to purge itself of dogmas with which it may at one time have been content: the use of evolution as an omnicompetent formula, the idea of the inevitability of progress, the certain perfectibility of man, the goal of a scientific Utopia. The critic of humanism cannot easily charge these essays with a facile optimism. There are indeed one or two traces (as in Kingsley Martin's piece) of the theme of Bertrand Russell's old essay on the Free Man's Worship: man's dignity shining in the face of calamity. But the general view prevails that with no sort of Utopianism the scientific outlook enables man both to do justice to his moral nature and to make the best possible job of overcoming the world's ills.

The Christian will want to criticize the book's critiques of Christianity. It would have been really helpful to be shown a fair picture of the Christian life at its noblest, with its otherworldly and thisworldly qualities, its sensitivity to suffering and its inner serenity, its philanthropy tinged with humility and penitence—and then to be shown where humanism is discontented and offers a better way. But instead we have in an essay entitled 'Morality—Supernatural or Social?', a very superficial and selective survey of Christian ethics through the centuries. Are not the social ethics of Romans 12 and the Epistles of St John very characteristic of Christianity and rooted in the mission of Christ himself? And we still get the allegation that the doctrine of reward in heaven is selfish, although as heaven is the perfection of persons in selfless love with one another and with God it is hard to see how any selfish motive or ambition can bring one a step nearer to heaven. Heaven is in essence the eradication of selfishness in the presence of God. Whenever Christians have thought otherwise, it has been a distortion of the teachings of the Beatitudes.

But the Christian who reads these essays will want to learn as well as to criticize. He will certainly learn that some of the stock religious criticisms of humanism are wide of the mark, and that to be a humanist is not necessarily to adhere to an all-embracing evolutionary theory, or to an optimism about society or human perfectibility. He will learn that too often Christians can practise a wrong kind of otherworldliness and can also be too ready to show the relevance of religion by dogmatizing on subjects which require the touch of the expert as well as the concern of the Christian. He will learn how ardently humanists are throwing themselves into the service of humanity in some of its distresses. He will learn how scientific method can aid some of the pastoral activities which are the Christian's traditional concern. He will learn to be cautious in speaking, à la Charles Snow, of the Two Cultures after reading an essay which searchingly criticizes the validity of that antithesis. Above all he will conclude that Christians are called upon to recover and represent under the conditions of today the spirit of Christian humanism which has been theirs in the past: a religion which finds the transcendent in the heart of human life and not apart from it and knows that no truth is to be feared since all truth is of God.

Alongside their pieces of anti-religious polemic the essays contain more than a few pleas that it is more urgent to serve the needs of humanity than to attack other theories about the meaning of that service. Christians will respond by being sure that wherever compassion, justice, and the care for persons are upheld they will join with others in the upholding of them whatever creed or non-creed is involved.

Yet amidst the self-criticism to which the book may lead him the Christian may draw from it a new confidence in what he believes. The book forces upon the mind the problem of human goodness. The essays neither explain goodness by an agreed ethical theory nor explain it away by any quasi-evolutionary one. They do not present us with a simple utilitarianism, partly because they are not so optimistic and partly because they see goodness as transcending utility. Nor on the other hand will they leave us with naked tragedy in the Greek manner as they have too much optimism for that. So, by their very freedom from theoretical solutions and by their plain avowal of goodness and their reverence for it, they are posing the question: Is goodness in human life a fortuitous product within the evolutionary process, or is it a *purpose* within and beyond that process? Is there something which man is *meant* to become? And when we say *meant* are we speaking of something with ultimate compulsive authority at once 'within' and 'beyond'?

Socrates was sure that he was *meant* to do and to be something in response to a meaning ultimate, within and beyond. If to speak thus is to make a leap which we call faith it is also, I believe, a rational understanding of human existence. 'We shall be like him, for we shall see him as he is.' Bethlehem tells how he whose likeness man is meant to become showed to us both the goal and the way, for in St Augustine's words: 'So deep has human pride sunk us that only divine humility can raise us.'

The Mystery of Life[1]

What is Man? He comes into existence in the evolution of the
mammal species on a little planet that revolves round the sun
amid the many thousand stars of the Milky Way. There is nothing
more wonderful in that than in any other part of what is 'rolled
round in earth's diurnal course, with rocks and stones and trees'.
But Man in his evolving history shows himself able to reflect
about the meaning of the process, and the meaning of himself,
and he is aware of certain concepts which have an absolute
claim upon him: beauty, truth, goodness. If he does not respond
to this claim wherever he is aware of it he experiences shame or
guilt. There is something Man is 'meant' to do and to be.

Whence have these seemingly absolute concepts come? Have
they been thrown up from the processes of the solar system or
the evolution of species like phenomena which come and go:
incidents in the story like the brontosaurus or the pterodactyl?
It is hard for men to think *that* when they find themselves rever-
encing these concepts and acting upon them as if it were they
that gave significance to the whole process of existence.

Again, are these concepts the outcome of some plan or contract
which Man has made for the ordering of his own happiness
upon his little planet? This might be so, were it not that conscience sometimes compels a man to do things which serve no
apparent useful end whatever, sacrificing home, country, happiness, utility, life itself, for the sake of a 'must' which is beyond
the temporal order. In other words, the source of the moral
life is beyond man's temporal existence, and the goal of the moral
life cannot be identified with any purely temporal ends.

Such is the road towards a belief in God and in immortality.
A baby 'matters' more than a million stars, more than the process
of evolution which led up to there being babies at all. He matters
because he will presently be able to respond with reverence and
love to *That* which gives meaning to the whole. His response defines
his duty in this life, but involves what is in turn meaningless

[1] This essay is reproduced by permission of the *Sunday Times*.

apart from a destiny beyond it. And, if the *That* to which he responds is akin to what is significant in himself, then he may name his goal not *That* but *He*.

I do not now pursue this argument further. I would rather describe a certain sort of man who illustrates what I have been saying. What is a *saint*? Saintliness is a known phenomenon. We call a man saintly not just because he is very good, nor yet because he is good and also religious. A saint is marked by a certain 'otherworldliness', by a serenity and happiness as of one who is 'yonder'—and yet there is no escapism, for he is very sensitive to the pains of his fellows and shares and bears them acutely. And he is marked also by an unselfconscious awareness of God which is the secret of an unusual humility: virtues and achievements cannot inflate him, for he ascribes them to their source, and a hidden sense of unworthiness (sometimes very painful) makes him yet more receptive of God's gifts. He is not surprised to find that there is 'a drop of poison in the chalice of the fullest secular happiness, a poison infused by the heavenly lover of all souls to prevent us from finding abiding happiness outside Himself'.

The Mystery of Life includes both its origin in the rudiments of the evolutionary process and its potentiality in the saintly life; and a scientific view of the world involves a view of its totality 'from the atom to the saint'. I believe that in this totality, with the emergence of new levels of being at many stages and with man as the climax, God discloses himself. And as the potentiality of animal life is seen in the remarkable animal called Man, so the potentiality of Man is seen in him whom the New Testament calls 'the New Man', Christ. Here the Creator discloses himself finally in one whose claim and character are such that he is rightly called 'the image of the invisible God'.

In Christ there is the disclosure of God, and also the restoration of Man: restoration—because he has been misusing his freedom. Among man's glorious characteristics is that measure of freedom whereby he may choose evil or good. His failing has been the pride or egoism with which he aggrandizes himself, using his powers with aggressive or complacent self-assertion instead of using them in humble dependence.

Hence it is that successive civilizations, full though they have been of moral and intellectual achievement, have had an inner sickness due to the disruption of man's right relation to his maker. The goal of the gospel of Christ is the restoration of that right relation, wherein the human race will reflect the Creator's own love in trustful dependence. This right relation is itself 'eternal life': it is here and now, but here and now cannot exhaust or define it.

Not seldom sensitive men and women have followed the line of belief which I have been describing; but have found it strained beyond endurance by the spectacle of suffering in the human race. So it is, until two facts are allowed to make the difference which they can make; and those facts are *Calvary* and the *Saints*. Calvary brings the conviction of a Creator not aloof but sharing in the conflict of his creatures and using suffering in the omnipotence of love. And the Saints show us the spirit of Calvary caught in human lives which show suffering transformed in love, sympathy, creativity. This is itself a part of the Mystery of Life, for that mystery includes not only the problem of evil but the astonishing problem of good.

Such is the way in which a Christian tries to face the Mystery of Life. The unlocking of some of the secrets heightens in turn the awe and wonder with which he contemplates the world's existence and his own.

Saints

Unless a grain of wheat falls into the earth and dies it remains alone, but if it dies it bears much fruit.   *John 12.24*

Tonight we are celebrating the light of Christ reflected in the saints.[1] This light is shining within a world darkened by shadows, for how terribly the word 'darkness' fits the conflicts of nations and races, the terrible contrasts of wealth in some countries and poverty and hunger in others, the unceasing unkindness of man to man and the frustrations of our civilization. Amidst this darkness we recapture the scene when our Lord comes near to the city of Jerusalem and weeps over it because it does not know the things which make for peace; and we may picture our Lord weeping over cities, towns, villages, countries at their present hour. But we also recall how our Lord, within the same city and on the night before the agonies of Good Friday, speaks to the disciples in the upper room: 'These things I have spoken to you, that my joy may be in you and that your joy may be full.' We forget neither his tears nor his joy, and both have been shared by his saints, for does not St Paul describe the Christian life 'as sorrowful, yet always rejoicing'?

It is amidst the bewilderment of the world that Christianity has something to say. And the question in the hearts of many of the bewildered is this: Is there in our divided and frustrated world anywhere a clue, a meaning, a pattern, a sovereignty, a way? And Christianity answers: Yes, there is a clue, a meaning, a pattern, a sovereignty, a way; and this is depicted in the parable of Jesus about the corn of wheat which dies in order to be fruitful. In the death and resurrection of Jesus there is disclosed the sovereign power by which evil is overcome and the divine purpose is shaped: life through death, losing life so as to find it. It is thus that God conquers evil. And wherever in the world there are lives which so live, there a light is shining reflecting Christ's own light, and there a trail is blazed.

[1] Sermon preached in All Saints', Margaret Street, on All Saints' Day, 1973.

So we salute the saints. These are, for a scientific inquirer into the universe, an exciting phenomenon, posing the questions: What do we make of them? and, What do they make of the world?

What are the saints like? How do we characterize them? It is not being *virtuous* that makes a saint: the Pharisees were very virtuous, and they and their virtues needed conversion. It is not *doing good* in the world that makes a saint; he does often do good, but so do many people whom we would never call saints. It is not success in the practice of *religion* which makes a saint. I expect you and I are pretty religious; but our religion, like every other part of us, needs converting. No, the saint is one who has a strange nearness to God and makes God real and near to other people. He embodies the parable of the corn of wheat that falls into the earth and dies. His virtues do not make him proud, for he is reaching out towards a perfection far beyond them and is humbled by this quest. His sins and failings, which may be many and bitter, do not cast him down, for the divine forgiveness humbles him and humbles him again. He shares and bears the griefs of his fellows and he feels the world's pains with a heightened sensitivity; but with that sensitivity he has an inner serenity of an unearthly kind which brings peace and healing to other people. This strange blending of humility, sorrow, and joy is the mark of a saint; and through him God is real and near.

But how varied are the saints. There are some of them whose lives are without actual poverty or physical suffering, but the Cross marks them, and the Cross is in their hearts and their minds rather than their bodies. And there are some of them who know grievous sickness and weakness of body, and there is in them, in a way that is at once lovely and frightening, a patience, a courage, a love, a strength, people of whom the world is not worthy. So tonight we salute the varied company of the saints in this Eucharist. They reflect Jesus in the world. They answer the question-mark of the bewildered who ask, Where is the clue? What is the goal? What is the world for? They show us what *we* are here for—'unless a grain of wheat falls to the earth and dies . . .'.

Now the immense claim, the claim that All Saints' Day points to the meaning of the world we live in, is a claim which Christianity addresses to all our faculties: our emotions, our will, you imagination, and our mind as well. Our response will be in the stirring of our emotions, the obedience of our will, the wonder of our imagination—and also the questing thought of our mind. It is a challenge to *think*, as well as to love, to obey, and to wonder. Therefore it seems to me very significant that the worship and sacramental life here in All Saints' Church goes hand in hand with the work of the Institute of Christian Studies across the road (in the building to be dedicated tonight) where truth is studied and explored and the questionings of the mind are faced. The phenomenon of the saints challenges us with searching questions about the world's meaning.

We picture again the scene on Palm Sunday. Jesus is in the city of Jerusalem, and amongst those who are eager to see him is a party of Greeks. They are searching for Jesus, and searching for truth. Whether they were precisely the 'intellectuals' we do not know, but searchers they certainly were. 'Sir, we would see Jesus.' And the answer which he gives is his answer to every seeker in every age: 'unless a grain of wheat falls to the earth and dies . . .'. It is a parable about the coming death of Jesus, a parable about the way of divine sovereignty, a parable about the clue to the world in which we live. Why was the world created? All Saints' Day gives the answer.

1 Signing the Common Declaration in Rome with Pope Paul VI, 1966
2 With soldiers in Belfast, 1974

3   With the Dalai Lama in London, 1973

Religion: Escape or Freedom?[1]

For centuries there have been those who have been anti-religion because they have been anti-God or anti-Christianity. In our own time, on the other hand, we have seen the new phenomenon of those who have been against religion in the name of God and of Christianity. There was Karl Barth's vigorous distinction between faith as an act which accepts God's gift by grace alone and religion as the human attempt to climb to God by pietistic exercises. There was Dietrich Bonhoeffer's thesis that religion belongs to man's immaturity and that man is now called to stand on his own feet and find God in the courageous encounters of human life without the childish props of religious practice. More conspicuous perhaps on this side of the Atlantic has been the theme of Harvey Cox in his book *The Secular City*.[2] As the God of the Bible led his people out by the hand of Moses into new adventures of serving him, so today God is leading his people away from serving him in religious cultus and into serving him by the practical activities of compassion and brotherhood in the technological culture which is itself the city of God's own making. Irrespective of these radical positions, however, there is among very many young Christians in England, and I cannot doubt in Canada too, the insistence that no Christianity is credible which does not express itself urgently in practical service and in grappling with the issues of poverty and race. Is there not a widespread Christian activism impatient of religious practice?

Yet another wind is also blowing. In the last year or two specially I have felt its presence, for not infrequently when I am asked to address young people the request comes not for a talk about race or poverty or social action but for a talk about meditation or contemplation. There is the hunger for mysticism, the longing to escape from the pressures of environment so that the self may realize itself in freedom, in touch with a reality

---

[1] A lecture given in Trinity College, Toronto, October 1971.
[2] London 1965.

Ec

that transcends. At the one end there is the revived interest in the mystical techniques of Eastern religions, at the other end there is the use of drugs in the quest of ecstatic experience. Amidst this mystical hunger Christianity is often written off, because its institutionalism inhibits spiritual adventure and because its activist preoccupations seem uninterested in religion. Here indeed is a judgement upon our Western Christendom if amidst our eagerness to enhance the second great commandment we have failed to be true to our own mystical tradition and to help those whose hunger is a religious one. Let me mention now in passing Harvey Cox's remarkable return to the religious dimension in his book *The Feast of Fools.*[1] In this striking book Cox draws out the role of festivity and fantasy as the ways in which man can live in the past and the future as well as in the present, and so can recover his own true timeless self. We find God in the dance before we can understand God in the dogma.

How can a mere theologian be of service to those upon whom these two winds are blowing powerfully today? He can try to see how they relate to the truth about God, man, and Christ. So let me make that attempt, not discouraged by Harvey Cox's remark, 'You cannot expect jester's theology from the archbishop's palace.'[2] Try we must, to see together in Christ the relation to God of which St Irenaeus said, 'The life of man is the vision of God', and the relation to the world of which the writer of the letter to Diognetus said, 'As the soul is in the body, so are the Christians in the world.'

Man exists to glorify his Creator. That is where we start. Glory and glorify are biblical words with very distinctive meaning. To glorify God is to reflect the radiance of God like a mirror, in a life of righteousness, justice, and compassion. But the nearer to God a man comes in so reflecting him, the more he is aware of his creaturely dependence, his unworthiness, his need for forgiveness, and the more he finds his joy in God himself in praise and gratitude. Those whom we call saints are men and women whose characters have been marked by the humility of the worshipping creature and the forgiven sinner. The goal of man created in God's image is heaven, for God in his love for man

[1] Cambridge, Mass. 1965.
[2] Op. cit., p. 13. Quotations from this book are by permission of Harvard University Press.

designs that man's fellowship with himself will be perfected and will be unceasing. St Augustine thus describes heaven: 'We shall rest and we shall see, we shall see and we shall love, we shall love and we shall praise, in the end which is no end.' *Rest*: we cease from our fussy busyness. *See*, because in thus resting our eyes will be opened and no longer blurred by our busyness, and we shall see God in his beauty and we shall see our fellows as they really are. Seeing, we shall not fail to *love*: to love our Creator and Saviour and to love our fellows selflessly. But, resting, seeing, and loving, our joy will be in him who is the giver and the goal, in God himself, and so the last word will be *praise*. It will be an end which is no end: it will be finality, beyond which nothing is more perfect, but a perfection within which there will be endless new adventures in resting, seeing, loving, and praising.

Meanwhile man, with the hope of heaven in his heart and with the hope of heaven giving the perspective of his present existence, is set to serve God within the world which God has created. With this world he is utterly involved, and his service of God is always through the world and not apart from it. In principle his relation to his fellow men is the stuff and substance of his worship of God; but in his present imperfection he is compelled to see in a certain duality, albeit a duality like the two sides of a coin, his worship of God and his service of man. Although we cannot expect jester's theology from an archbishop's palace I recall some words of William Temple, who was indeed both a jester and a theologian: 'It is sometimes said that conduct is supremely important, and worship helps it. The truth is that worship is supremely important, and conduct tests it.' Isn't that right? The priority for man is his enjoyment of God for God's sake, in whom is the perfection of all that can be perfect; an enjoyment that can never be selfish as it is outgoing love responding to outgoing love; God can never be treated as if he were the means towards ends greater than himself. But because God is righteous there is no true worship of him that is not immediately reflected in the love and service of our neighbour in society. Our love and service of our neighbour, however, will be saved from being patronizing or possessive as in the doing of it we are humbled by God's forgiveness and by our knowing that God's glory is the goal of what we are trying to do.

It is on the ground of these main theological principles about God and man, the Church and the world, that we need to see, to assess, to learn from, and (if need be) to correct the trends both of an activism which is often anti-religious and of neo-mysticism in its various forms.

The anti-religious attitude which has most force and intelligibility is, I think, that derived from Bonhoeffer: the idea that religion can keep men childish, dependent upon pious exercises as a kind of prop, whereas (it is supposed) God would prefer his children to grow up, to stand on their own feet, to forget the conscious reference of everything to their Father, and to find God rather in the midst of the courageous facing of life's encounters and conflicts. Is there a moral for us? Yes, perhaps it is this: that we ought, while continuing to believe in man's creatureliness, to emphasize also his vocation to grow through sonship into being a fellow-worker with God and thus to share as a son in the Father's creative process. Too often our piety can fall short of that, and can indeed remain childish. But let man grow into his role as mature son and fellow-creator; he will still be liable to sin, and will need at times to be prostrate before the holy and forgiving God; and the greatness of God is such that the bravest and strongest will find themselves little in his presence. It is one thing to be childish, with a religion which never grows up. It is another thing to be childlike, with a religion which matures into a manly independence and yet discovers an ever-deepening dependence upon God as our origin and our goal.

Much, however, of the anti-religious trend is, I believe, a reaction from misleading ideas about the divine transcendence. God's transcendence does not mean that he is away from the world, living in some kind of space outside it. His beyondness is the beyondness of one who is here, everywhere, present in every human situation. It is here, everywhere, in every human situation that we know God, as One who is always here and always beyond here. Perhaps the older Christian spirituality tended too much to think of our serving God in the world in one direction, and then going off in another direction to find the God who transcends. We sometimes hear the phrase 'new spirituality'. I take it to mean that while God is indeed beyond we are to find his beyondness in and amongst life's daily circumstances. There will still be retreat, still withdrawal; but it will be a retreat and withdrawal from the surface of life so as to recollect the God who is the reality within it and beyond it.

Now for the other trend, 'neo-mysticism'. Amidst the pressures and strains of life there is the longing of the self to realize itself by escaping from the dominance of environment. There are many cults which offer such an escape, with an experience of a heightening of the faculties and a realization of the self in greater power of its own or of something beyond the self. But it is important to ask what is the reality which is experienced, and what is the effect not only upon the sensations but upon the life and character of the person who has the experience. There is an old story of a man who was had up before the magistrate for being drunk. The magistrate asked, 'Why do you get drunk like this?', and the man replied, 'You see, your worship, it's the shortest way out of Manchester.' Alcohol, drugs, the mystical techniques of various religions, may be the shortest way out of Manchester, or out of Toronto. But it matters very much where you get to, and what you are like when you come back.

Mysticism in the proper sense is an intense realization of God within the self and the self embraced within God in vivid nearness. It is a phenomenon known in a number of religions, and in those religions very similar language is used in describing the experience. There is deep darkness, the darkness of not knowing; and there is light with flashes in which the self knows the unknowable terribly near and knows itself as never before. Now through the centuries Christian teaching has emphasized that the significant thing is not just the mystic experience in itself but its place and its context within the whole life of a Christian. The experience is given by God sometimes to one who seeks God in a life of humility and charity, turned towards the righteousness as well as the beauty of God. And the effect of the experience of mystic union, sometimes described as 'passive contemplation', is not to cause the person to long to have the experience again but to long to serve God and to do his will. Those who have had mystic experience will not want to tell everyone about it: they will have a longing to serve God in daily life, for in his *will* is our peace.

Mystic experience is given to some. But contemplation is for all Christians. Allow me a word about that prayer which is indeed for all of us. The prayer of Jesus our high priest is classically described in the sentence 'he ever lives to make intercession for us'. Now the Greek word which is here, and elsewhere, translated 'intercede' does not mean to speak or to plead or to make requests or petitions: it means to *meet* someone, to *be with* someone in relation to or on behalf of others. Jesus is with the Father, for us. And our own prayer means essentially our being with God, putting ourselves in his presence, being hungry and thirsty for him, wanting him, letting heart and mind and will move towards him; with the needs of our world on our heart. It is a rhythmic movement of our personality into the eternity and peace of God and no less into the turmoil of the world for whose sake as for ours we are seeking God. If that is the heart of prayer, then the contemplative part of it will be large. And a Church which starves itself and its members in the contemplative life deserves whatever spiritual leanness it may experience.

Now it is easy to assert that neither the wind of activism nor the wind of neo-mysticism exhausts the truth of God in Christ, and that either wind may be misleading, and that Christian truth corrects both and is greater than both. Yet *spiritus ubi vult spirat*, and just now there are on the frontiers of organized Christianity groups and societies claiming Christian inspiration, some of them intent upon the radical practising of Christian brotherhood and the service of human needs, some of them intent upon the reception of a religious experience more vivid than anything which institutional Christianity seems able to offer. Institutional Christianity can fulfil a mission of help only if it will see itself under judgement and will learn from the upheavals of the time. A prosperous religious culture with a deadened conscience about race or poverty is a monstrosity which brings its revenge. So too does an ethical and activist religion which starves itself by its neglect of contemplation. It is of our contemporary Christian religious civilization that Harvey Cox says this, not without justice, in *The Feast of Fools*: 'It has resulted in a deformed man whose sense of a mysterious origin and a cosmic destiny has nearly disappeared.'[1]

In the same book Cox characterizes the two types as the new mystics and the new militants. The former find in 'celebrating

[1] Op. cit., p. 15.

life' the recapture of the festivity and the fantasy and the escape
from the rule of convention, of nationalism, and of the present.
The new militants have not 'contemplation' but 'participation'
as their key word. Giving instances of how the two streams
sometimes flow into one another Cox adds:

> Just as Catholics and Protestants need each other in the Church,
> so do the celebrators of life today and the seekers of justice
> tomorrow need each other in the world. Celebration without
> politics becomes effete and empty. Politics without celebration
> becomes mean and small. The festive spirit knows how to
> toast the future, drink the wine, and break the cup. They all
> belong together.[1]

But if these two kinds of people need each other, they need
most of all what we all need—Christ's own answer in his body
and his blood. It is time that we turned to the night in which
Christ was betrayed. When he took the bread and gave thanks and
broke it he gathered into one the fragments of truth and insight
about which we have been thinking.

Recall the scene. The Lord Jesus is with the apostles at supper.
They are celebrating—celebrating as at every Passover time
the goodness of the God who had freed their nation from
slavery in Egypt, and celebrating also the hope of heaven and
of good things to come. The sad and sombre setting of imminent
death for Jesus and an unknown future for the disciples could
not dim the joy of celebrating. And now our Lord speaks.
'This is my body, given for you': he breaks the loaf and bids
them eat. 'This is my blood, of the covenant, poured out for
you': and he bids them drink. Body broken, blood poured—it
means Jesus himself, Jesus in his death. On the next day he is
going to die, and the death on a mound outside the city gate
will be an event outside them—outside them, to watch perhaps
from near, perhaps from a distance—but outside them. But,
eat! drink! The death is to become not only outside them, but
within them, something to be shared. It will be food to them:
it will be drink to them. It will be within them, part of them,
that by which they live. So some years later the apostle says
to the Christians of Corinth: 'The bread which we break, is it

[1] Op. cit., p. 120.

not a participation in the body of Christ; the cup which we drink, is it not a participation in the blood of Christ?'

Not all Christians are called to actual martyrdom, but all are called to something of which martyrdom is the external sign—the sharing in the self-giving, the offering, the selflessness of the Lord. Thus in the Eucharist Christ crucified and risen does his mighty work of drawing his people to participate more and more in his own life of living through dying. In Johannine terms the glory seen in Calvary and Easter, the glory wherewith the Son glorifies the Father eternally, is given to the disciples to be glory in them.

Now through the centuries different aspects of the many-sided mystery of the Eucharist have been dwelt upon in doctrine and devotion, and sometimes—as is the wont of Christian perversity—the various aspects have been used defensively, divisively: whether the metaphysical relation of the Lord's presence to the elements of bread and wine, or the relation of the sacrifice of praise and thanksgiving to the sacrifice of the Cross. Today the antitheses and the contrasts more in evidence are those which relate to those issues of religion and non-religion, of the sacred and the common, about which we have been thinking this evening. There are those who would emphasize that the Christians are celebrating a meal, with their fellowship with one another in homeliness, and their participation in the world they are serving. There are those on the other hand who remind us that we are making the memorial of the Crucifixion of the Lord and that our fellowship is with the saints in heaven. Let me suggest to you a line of thought which tries to express the whole reality.

The author and the agent in the Eucharist is the Word of God. The Word is proclaimed in the scripture lections and in the preaching. Then the same Word, who is Jesus, blesses the loaf and the cup, and invites and commands us. If we respond and receive on our knees nothing is more fitting to the awe and reverence of adoration; but if we respond and receive standing—as was probably the ancient custom—nothing is more fitting as the sign of obedience, ready to go and to save. For Jesus the Word feeds us so that we may be increasingly his own Body in the world to share with him in his work of the world's re-creation. He does not feed us in order to draw us away with him into a separated realm of religion, but to draw us into participation with him in the work of moulding the world into his own likeness.

This aspect of the Eucharist has been powerfully drawn out by Dr Arthur Vogel, formerly Professor at Nashotah House and now Bishop of West Missouri, in his book *Is the Last Supper Finished? Secular Light on a Sacred Meal.*[1] Vogel, who is among the most creative of contemporary Anglican theologians in the United States, writes:

> For Christians, the creation of God's world is still going on through men, and Providence is the name of the process.

> The Christians' liturgy is to continue God's creation of the world through their incorporation into his Body-Word, Jesus Christ. In God's community his people receive his meaning (the Word) in order to manifest it through their bodily lives wherever they are in the universe.

> If the nature of the Eucharist is as I have described it, narrow provincialism of any kind is impossible in Christian living. We cannot participate in Christ's self-giving death through the eucharistic liturgy, and then try to protect ourselves by his food. In the mystical and sacramental bodies of Christ God is among us still doing his work, i.e. creating the world.

> Through the Eucharist we are extensions of Christ's vulnerability, sustained by the food of his victory; we are not guards placed at the door of his anteroom to protect him from profanation or contact with the world.

One last quotation, to excite your interest in a most valuable book.

> The Word of God cannot be read or heard as if it were past, abstract, finished or something to be used by us. By rejoicing in it we give ourselves so completely to it that we in one sense become it; to the extent that we become it we are its proclamation.

St Augustine said of old, '*accedit verbum pani, et fit sacramentum*'. Add together the Word and the Loaf, and the Sacrament is there. It is a sacrament which sustains us to be ourselves Christ's

[1] Copyright, 1968, Sheed and Ward, Inc., New York.

body in the re-creation of the world. In the sacrament we are one with the risen Christ and we are united with the saints in heaven, with the Mother of our Lord and the holy angels; but as love is one and indivisible the Eucharist is the gate of heaven only as being also the gate through which we go out into the service of the world. So in this sacrament the *neo-militant* is given the humility with which alone his warfare will be Christian, the *activist* is called to silence for a space in the contemplation of a great mystery, the *neo-mystic* is shown that the one reality worth possessing is Christ crucified, and *all of us* are allowed to celebrate the sorrow and the joy of Christ.

To Pray is to Serve[1]

And he dreamed, and behold a ladder set up on the earth, and the top of it reached to heaven.   *Genesis 28.12*

Within the family of Christ's people there are many divers vocations. Many, indeed the majority, of Christian men and women are called by God to marriage, the family, and the home. Through the centuries, Christ has called some to the religious life in the threefold vows of poverty, chastity, obedience. Here is an intensely evangelical part of Christianity, rooted in the gospel story. Jesus calls some to literal poverty. Jesus spoke of the call to celibacy as given to those able to receive it. And while all Christians must obey, Christ's call to poverty and to chastity has with it necessarily a very distinctive obedience.

And as to the religious vows. These are not presumptuous. These are not a piece of Pelagian self-determination. Rather the vows of religion mean the total acceptance of the call of God and the gift from God—an acceptance 'by faith alone' and 'by grace alone'. To God alone be the glory.

Now there was perhaps never a time when the religious life was more significant in Christendom and in the world than today. If God calls and if God disposes gifts, the call and the gifts are true and valid in their own right because they are God's; but yet we are able to see how God's call and God's gifts can answer the problems and needs of different epochs in history. Today there is the love of pleasure, self-pleasing, wilfulness, the belief that life is best with no authority at all, and it is against that that the call to obedience in the religious life is so very significant as a witness to the truth of God. Today the love of money, and the spirit of getting and grabbing is widespread, and against that the joy of poverty in Christian vocation is so very significant. And today, too, lust and self-expression, and self-expression as an unthinking ideal, are widespread, and

[1] Address at the consecration of the new chapel at St Mary's Abbey, West Malling, 20 June 1966.

against that the call to the beauty and joy of chastity is very significant also.

And as to the life of a religious community. Here its stability and its permanence has a telling, divine meaning. Human life flits, these days, from one excitement to another, from one novelty to another, a little of this and a little of that, and the bondage to the passing moment is widespread. And hence a witness to God is borne by the stability of a Christian home and a Christian marriage, 'those whom God has joined together, let no man put asunder', a union of lives 'until death us do part'. So, too, a witness to God is borne by the stability of a religious community. It stands for the permanence of the vocation in its members, but it stands also for a witness to things that are not shaken, to truths and ideals which are not of any one age but reach across the centuries, a ladder set up and its top reaches to heaven.

Today our minds go back to the year 1090 when Gundulf, bishop of Rochester, first founded St Mary's Abbey at West Malling. Gundulf was a monk of Bec and Lanfranc had been his prior and Anselm one of his contemporaries. And the see of Canterbury, no less than the see of Rochester, has a share in the old history of West Malling and a joy in the great event of today. After the establishment of the convent by Gundulf it endured for four and a half centuries and the Benedictine Rule was followed within its walls, and God's servants worshipped here and lived the common life, and it was no dream that a ladder was set up on the earth and the top of it reached to heaven.

Today the lovely Gate House, the old West Tower, and much beside, stand from those older days, a token of the things that are not shaken. Today, in our Anglican communion, we thank God that through a century and more, the religious life has been reviving and growing, and amidst that revival the Benedictine way has been followed here in West Malling from early in the present century. Today we all, Christians from near and far, Christians not only of the Anglican obedience but of other Christian communions too—Orthodox, Roman Catholic, Protestant—join here in giving great thanks to God. We thank God for the revival of the religious life. We thank God for the Abbey here at West Malling, for its worship and its service. We thank God for the building of this lovely chapel and for its consecration, and in its consecration we offer the future into God's good, firm, and loving hands.

Now the Benedictine way is a way of worship and work; *laborare est orare, orare est laborare.* As such, the Benedictine way is an epitome of Christian life itself. Now, ideally, work and worship are utterly one. Every deed of service of the Christian hand or the Christian brain is a lifting up of the soul to God, and the top of the ladder reaches to heaven. Equally, every lifting up of the soul to God in adoration is a profound service of the human race, and the ladder is indeed set upon this earth. But in our present inevitable imperfection our lives have to be divided, divided into those times which we call 'saying our prayers', and the times which we call 'getting on with our work'. And this dichotomy, present in all Christians in the world, appears no less in the religious life; and hence in the history of the religious life there are communities which use the phrase 'the mixed life'. For them prayer, worship, is the supreme priority; the Liturgy and the Office and personal prayer come always first, and first unshakeably. But besides the prayer a community may be dedicated to particular works in education or evangelism, or the care of the sick or the poor, or many kinds of service to humanity and to human crafts.

Here at West Malling is an abbey where the work is not prayer plus this, plus that, and plus the other, but where the work is prayer, plus prayer, plus prayer, plus prayer. The prayer is itself the work, and the service of the world is itself the prayer offered to the most high God on the world's behalf. And this means an apartness, an apartness like the apartness of our Lord in the Judean desert: praying and fighting on behalf of us all, on behalf of the human race. It is an apartness, a being with God, but always on behalf of the human race with its sins, its joys, and its sorrows.

The apartness, as all Christian apartness, must be real and costly. The nearness must be real and costly too. So it is that wherever there is a community, a family of Christian people dedicated supremely to prayer on behalf of the world and to prayer on behalf of all of us—the sinful, struggling members of the Christian Church in our various offices and callings—we know that in that community and in that family there is care and help and love and we are understood and prayed for and cared for and helped very mightily. And so it is that many individual men and women and children in the Church and beyond the Church know that here, as in many another house devoted to prayer, their sins and their troubles are cared for and they are being greatly helped. Similarly many distresses in the Church, in this country, and in the wider world are being likewise helped and served. The door of prayer towards heaven, towards the heart of God, is always a door of love into the world of human needs.

One special need and cause engages day by day and night by night the prayers of the family in this place. This is the sharing in the prayer of our Lord, *ut omnes unum sint*. Christians—Orthodox, Roman Catholic, Anglican, Protestant—not seldom find their way here, to bring their prayer and to have their prayers strengthened by the ceaseless prayer, *ut omnes unum sint*, that persists here by day and by night. Here in this Christian family there is perhaps something of the spirit of the Orthodox East; but the Benedictine way is, of course, inseparable from the Latin West. The Liturgy is primitive in shape and in spirit, going behind the sophisticated developments in the worship of Christendom; and the love of holy Scripture makes the Abbey one with every Christian community in the world which in simplicity loves the Bible. Thus the prayer that all may be one, by night, by day, goes on with wisdom and knowledge and understanding, as well as with love; and the prayer is indeed a ladder, and the top of it reaches to heaven.

But the ladder of Christian prayer not only reaches to heaven and rests most firmly on earth. More than that, it unites heaven and earth very closely, because the ladder is Jesus, the Incarnate Lord. In him, through him, we share today in the prayers and praises of the blessed saints in heaven. In him, through him, we touch with our prayers the sins and sorrows of mankind. And in him, through him, our prayers shall be made one in him, as he is in the Father in the bond of the Holy Ghost. To whom be glory, praise, and thanksgiving from angels and from men, now and for evermore.

The Message of R. M. Benson

Always bearing about in the body the dying of Jesus, that the life
also of Jesus may be manifested in our body   *2 Corinthians 4.10*

as sorrowful, yet alway rejoicing   *2 Corinthians 6.10*

On the Feast of St John the Evangelist 1866 three men said
in the presence of one another:

In the name of the Father, and of the Son and of the Holy
Ghost, Amen. I, Richard Meux Benson, I, Charles Grafton, I,
Samuel Wilberforce O'Neill, promise and vow to Almighty
God, the Father the Son and the Holy Ghost before the whole
company of Heaven and before you my fathers, that I will
live in celibacy, poverty and obedience as one of the Mission
Priests of St John the Evangelist to my life's end, so help
me God.

So began the Cowley Fathers. Today, one hundred years after,
we thank God for the event;[1] for the calling of his three servants
to this venture, for the wise sympathy of Bishop Wilberforce
which from the first bound together the Community and the
Church, for the continuity of the Cowley Fathers through the
years 'always bearing about in the body the dying of Jesus that
the life also of Jesus may be manifested in our body'.

I speak today about the founder: not in nostalgia for a hero
of the past but as listening with you to one who speaks to us
urgently today about our Christian calling.

Richard Meux Benson was born of wealthy parents in 1824. He
was a gay and sociable undergraduate at Christ Church, a conscientious Senior Student of the same foundation, and soon
after his ordination he became Vicar of Cowley. From early
manhood he had some of the characteristics of the Tractarians:
the conviction that the Christian life is a hidden life, the conviction
of an austere call to holiness and of the unity between holiness

---

[1] This address was given in the Community Church at Cowley, 7 May 1966.

and dogmatic truth. Yet there was in Benson something a little different, the key to part of his greatness. This 'something a little different' lay, I believe, in his character as a theologian.

Benson's theology came to him through the absorption into him of the holy Scriptures and the Fathers. His love for them was no doubt learned from Pusey. But Benson was never a disciple to a master, as Liddon was to Pusey, or Church to Newman, or Kingsley to Arnold. He seldom quoted other writers, and he did not follow leaders, or schools, or systems. He absorbed. And without a great deal of technical scholarly equipment he disciplined himself in the New Testament in depth and wholeness. As a result, there was in him, far more I think than in other nineteenth-century teachers, a continual glimpse of the whole mystery of Christ, born, crucified, risen, and ascended, as the heart of theology and the heart of the Church.

Benson's theology appears not only in his published books but also in his letters. Here the theme recurs of the unity of the Passion and Resurrection of our Lord. The Passion is always seen in glory, and the Resurrection is always seen as the victory of one who died. This is no worship of a *past* mystery, for Christ ascended from us in order to be in us through the Paraclete, so that his dying and rising become ours. Nor is this a doctrine of Christ worship, for in all that Christ does he glorifies the Father and leads us to the Father. Benson held together these aspects of the truth with a rare consistency and sensitivity, and an awareness that here is the meaning not only of the gospel but of the Church as well. Not for Benson was the crudity into which that great man J. M. Neale once lapsed in the lines 'and so the Holy Church is here, although the Lord is gone', nor the correct yet one-dimensional view of the Church as the extension of the Incarnation, since Ascension no less than Incarnation is at the heart of the Church whose members are already ascended with Christ. Benson's belief in Christ as the very life of the Church led to his particular emphasis upon Holy Baptism. His words are well known: 'In Western Christendom the Holy Eucharist has so entirely overshadowed Holy Baptism that the food of our life is made to be a gift greater than the life which it sustains.'

Inevitably Benson was more at home with the Fathers than with the Schoolmen. He sometimes spoke severely of the Schoolmen's tendency to confuse God as the truth with men's rational

4 With the
Oecumenical Patriarch
Athenagoras I
in London, 1967

5　The opening service of Trinity Institute, New York, 1974

apprehension of the truth. He sometimes seems near to F. D. Maurice's sense of theology as the truth of the living God in contrast with men's systems of apprehending truth, whether Catholic or Evangelical or Liberal. Yet Benson was far from Maurice on one important matter. He could not blend redemption and creation in the way that Maurice did, because for him the contrast and conflict between the redeemed order and the world was sharp and persistent. Loving God, hating the world: dying to the world, rising with Christ—that was always at the heart. It is when the man of faith dies to the world's standards, ambitions, ideas of achievement, ideas of success, that he knows the joy of Christ. So he says: 'Until people realize the antagonism between Christ and the world, they cannot come to Him to be saved out of the world.' Again, 'We must learn to find our joy, our whole joy in Jesus alone, before we can find true joy in anything else that he can give. . . . We are too content to receive Jesus as an addition to ourselves.'

With this theology Benson was utterly concerned with the Church's mission to the world. Without relaxing the deep antagonism between Church and world the Church must involve itself in the life of the people wherever it may be. In India Father O'Neill and his companions were sharing a completely Indian life amongst Indians: cooking, eating, living in the Indian way, stepping right out of Europe into India. It is in some of Benson's letters to the Brothers in India that we see his thoughts about the Church's mission. The conversion of India, he says, is part of the Father's gift to the Son; and it is for us to be ready to receive in the Son's name and be conformed to the suffering whereby he receives the gift. Besides the hiddenness and the loneliness inherent in the work of mission there is a heroic patience. Wait, wait, wait, Benson keeps saying. 'We must evangelise with the cross of many a wearing year of resultlessness, and yet feel that our labour is not vain in the Lord.' 'One must learn one's own nothingness in a heathen city, as the power through which that city will be converted.' 'We must lie hid for a long time resultless, if our work is to grow in the end.' 'We don't make things grow by digging up the earth in which the seed is contained.' It is in Benson's mind a work partly visible on earth and partly wrought in heaven. As the Church dies to the world in pain and patience souls are won; and Christ knows,

Fc

as we do not know, whether he will save by many or by few, whether he will save rapidly or slowly.

It is not surprising that, springing from this theology, some of Benson's practical counsels are as witty as they are stern, as sympathetic as they are severe. I quote at random a warning not to measure Christian progress by church buildings. 'Certainly the fine churches of the present day are a remarkable sign of the times. I sometimes wonder how far it is a healthy sign. One is rather fearful lest the hardness of the stone should be a symbol of the hearts of the worshippers, although the beauty of form may symbolize the loveliness of divine truth.' 'Handsome churches seem to me to be a necessary end of our day where there is a Christian population, and as a matter of fact they have sprung up rather as the sepulchre than as the home of the living Church.'

I must bring to an end this sketch of Benson's teaching. He saw the calling of the Cowley brotherhood, and indeed the calling of the whole Church, as 'the contemplative gazing to God and doing battle with Satan which is the essential characteristic of all Christian life'.

Now what is the message of all this for today? When all is said and done, despite the otherworldliness and the austerity of the man and his message, its form could not help belonging to a kind of nineteenth-century religious mental culture, a kind of religious mental culture which is not and perhaps cannot be ours. Perhaps therefore we best begin to apply his message to our times if we take seriously his repeated encouragement to Christians in India to be with the people, in the people, of the people. He would surely tell us in the England of the 1960s that we as Christians must be with the people, in the people, discovering new forms in which the life in Christ is lived, and stripping away what is irrelevant to that task.

Yet in this task of putting the Church's life right into the context of secular man, we can still listen to the warning of Benson that we do this in an authentically Christian way, with Christian joy in the doing of it, only if there is deep in us the awareness of the conflict between Christ and the world as the New Testament sees it. Identification with the world goes with a real death to the world unless we are to be apostates from the scandal, and the power, of the Cross.

So too Benson would warn us, when we look for the Church's renewal through the Church's more effective encounter with the community, not to confuse Christ's criteria of success or failure with our own criteria of success or failure. When Benson speaks of 'evangelizing with the cross of many a wearing year of resultlessness and yet feeling that our labour is not vain in the Lord' he is a good deal nearer to the Gospels than is the kind of idea that if we toil in a place for a few years with no very visible result everything must be wrong and hopeless.

No part of Benson's message, however, is more important for us than what he says, again and again, about joy and its place in the Christian and the Church. After all, 'the fruit of the Spirit is love, joy . . .', and to be without joy may be as big an apostasy as to be without love. 'In our modern Christianity', Benson says—and it is as true of 1966 as of 1866—'in our modern Christianity how little there is of that ecstatic joy which fills St Paul's heart and inspired his writings.' But the secret of joy is not to moan because things go badly, in the hope that through moaning the way to success may be found so that after success some reason for joy may be provided. The secret of joy is in the death to self and in the joy of Christ alike in success or in failure, and without that joy the world will not be won.

Christmas 1973

You know the grace of our Lord Jesus Christ, that though he was rich for your sake he became poor, that you through his poverty might be rich.   *2 Corinthians 8.9*

Today the joy of Christmas shines in a world which is darkened by sadness.[1] In this country we are experiencing trials unknown to us in time of peace, and anxieties about trials which may yet be coming. But there is something very real about this Christmas. We are brought face to face with the reality of *Bethlehem*. We have often had romantic thoughts about the stable where Christ was born—but today we can better think what it was like: a stable, no warmth, no heat, small comfort, a rough and cold birthplace. So too we are brought face to face with the reality of *the world we live in*: we are, for example, stirred to remember those in this country who are homeless; it was so last Christmas, it was so the Christmas before that—and now perhaps the reality hits our minds. And we remember that in some countries there are many people who have very little to eat, getting today perhaps a few mouthfuls while we have our dinner. Then there is another kind of reality which meets us this Christmas—those *human qualities* which can shine out in a time of trouble: comradeship, courage, kindness, and the readiness of people to make sacrifices for one another. How real indeed are these gifts of human goodness, and they are gifts of the God of Bethlehem who is their source, the God who took human flesh in the stable is the God from whose store of love humanity's gifts of love are drawn.

It was no doubt with Bethlehem in mind that St Paul wrote, in the words I have chosen for my text, that Jesus Christ *became poor*. The stable is the symbol of Christ's poverty. Now we ought not to exaggerate or to sentimentalize the poverty of Christ. There is no suggestion in any of the Gospels that Christ was ever destitute or in abject penury. Joseph had a trade, and Jesus

[1] Sermon preached in Canterbury Cathedral, Christmas Day, 1973.

grew up in the security of a happy home. We know that he shared in social pleasure, and enjoyed at times being both a guest and a host. But the characteristic which gave him the title poor was *simplicity*. Again and again he struck the note of simplicity. He did without many things that people crave for. None did he criticize more severely than those who hankered after more and more possessions and those who were preoccupied with money. The worth of a man's life, he insisted, does not consist in the things that he has; his worth is not increased by piling up and piling up. People matter more than things, for people have an eternal destiny. And those who do not fuss about their standards of living and their luxuries are free to love one another, serve one another, and enjoy one another as people.

We remember indeed that Christ hated injustice and oppression, and we as Christians will be uncompromisingly against injustice, amongst ourselves and in the wider world. But today let the Christmas message of simplicity come home to us. Let us reverse the processes of looking for higher and higher standards, and resolve that enough is enough and luxuries are unnecessary, that many of us can be as happy or happier with less. Christ became poor, Christ chose the way of simplicity; and if we follow him he promises us riches of his own, riches of a happiness and a brotherhood shared with one another and with him.

'Though he was rich, for your sake he became poor, that you through his poverty might be rich.' Let me draw out St Paul's imagery. How was our Lord ever rich? He was the Son of God, rich in the attributes and powers of Divinity, very God of very God. Those were his riches. How did he become poor? By coming to share in the limitations, the frustrations, the hard realities, of our human life, our pains and sorrows and even our death. The imagery of Christ's riches and Christ's poverty is a vivid picture of the Incarnation, when the Word became flesh and dwelt among us. But while it is one thing to accept the doctrine of the Incarnation as the imagery of St Paul, no less than the imagery of St John, expresses it, it is another thing to grasp its moral message and to live by it, the message of simplicity and self-sacrifice. Christ's glory was to be humble himself and serve us all by his life and death. Let it be the glory of those who at this time have *more* to shoulder burdens and help those who have *less*. Let it be the glory of all of us to bear

one another's trials and find a new outgoing service and comradeship. Let it be the glory of a country to serve other countries,
the glory of Europe to serve the rest of the world as best it can.
Christ gave himself to us to enable us to give ourselves to one
another. That is the message of Bethlehem to a world in trouble.

'Being rich he became poor, that you through his poverty
might be rich.' The riches which Christ would share with us
are his glory, his power, and his joy.

Christ's glory is the self-giving love seen in his life and death.
He would share that with us, and he indeed shares it with us in
the Blessed Sacrament today. Christ's power was the kind of
power men found it hard to understand: not the power of privilege and lording it over people, but the more subtle power of
loving influence, of the winning of minds and consciences to the
truth. He would share that power with us, as we forsake the
kinds of power which he rejected. Christ's joy is something which
Christians have often shared and known. While the joys of
fame and wealth and luxury prove shallow and passing, there
is in unselfish brotherhood, even amidst trials and pains, a joy
that is deep and lasting. We who are Christians are called to make
Christ's glory our own and Christ's power our own. And with
these gifts there comes his joy. Let that joy be ours this Christmas,
and we shall be spreading it around us in the year, indeed the
years, which lie ahead.

> Yea, Lord, we greet thee,
> Born this happy morning.

Come to Bethlehem once again. See the stable, see the child.
And knowing that he is God made Man, knowing that he who
was rich has become poor for us, we can kneel in the darkness
and the cold which is the symbol of our blind and chilly human
race and say with a grasp we may never have had before the
doxology at the end of the Lord's Prayer: 'yours is the kingdom,
and the power, and the glory for ever.'

2
Church and Unity

The Fire of Pentecost[1]

There appeared to them tongues like flames of fire, dispersed
among them and resting on each one.   *Acts 2.3, NEB*

Whitsunday is a great day because it helps us to answer the
question: Where is God? We know God above us and around
us, our Creator and our Father. We know God uniquely revealed
to us in Jesus, and we recall the words, 'he that has seen me has
seen the Father'. But for the first Christians both those kinds of
knowledge of God were inseparable from a power within them
which Jesus had promised, the power described as Holy Spirit,
mighty but intimate and personal too. Their continuing faith
in the God revealed in Jesus was inseparable from God now
within themselves. Today we join with Christians everywhere
in rejoicing in the God who is within.

Recall the event of the first Whitsunday. The company of
disciples are together in the city of Jerusalem. Suddenly they
heard, they felt, they saw something happening: overwhelming
in effect, convincing to their minds and consciences. The words
of the New English Bible are vivid: 'a noise like a strong driving
wind . . . , tongues like flames of fire resting on each one'. Convinced that here was a supernatural power invading them, they
spoke to the crowds with boldness about Jesus Christ, and many
people were cut to the heart and asked to be baptized and admitted
to the fellowship of the Church. It was a fellowship of people
who looked 'up' as they thought of Jesus as Lord, exalted to
heaven, and who looked 'within' as they knew that divine
power was there, sustaining their faith in Jesus and enabling
them to dare great things for him.

Now the strange things which happened at Pentecost provide
for all time the symbols whereby Christians describe the actions
of the Holy Spirit in Christian lives. The effects of God's actions
are seen in human behaviour: the actions themselves, in minds,
hearts, and consciences, are describable in symbol alone. On the

[1] Preached in Canterbury Cathedral on Whitsunday, 1963.

day of Pentecost the gale of wind was felt, the tongues like fire were seen. But in the souls of men and women through the centuries what do the Wind and the Fire denote? The Wind no doubt means overwhelming, unseen power, the imagery used in our Lord's conversation with Nicodemus. The Fire, I ask you now to think what it denotes. What does Fire tell us about the Holy Spirit?

Think of yourself on a cold, dark night, like many we have had in this past winter. You slip into a room. No lights are on. It seems dark and cold. But presently just a little light, just a little warmth reaches you. You move on. A fire is burning.

First, you begin to see. In the brightness of the fire you notice in the room shapes, forms, outlines. If someone else is in the room you see his face, reflecting the fire. The Holy Spirit enables you to see, and to see like a Christian—perceiving things as they really are in the eyes or the mind of Jesus, perceiving people as they really are with the light of Jesus upon them, perceiving meanings and purposes instead of shapeless confusion, perceiving what a Christian ought to be doing. Remember the words in the *Veni Creator*:

> enable with perpetual light
> the dullness of our blinded sight

Remember too the words in the Whitsunday Collect where we pray that the Holy Spirit may give us 'right judgment in all things'. The Holy Spirit keeps the light of Jesus glowing in us: that is how we may see as Christians should see.

Next, the fire as you approach it gives you warmth. Warm itself, it makes you warm. So the warmth of the love of God within you can warm your heart to love him in response. This is not a matter of sentiment only. The very love of God can penetrate you and warm your faculties to love him. So we say:

> thy blessed unction from above
> is comfort, light and fire of love,

and an old Christian writer speaks of *Incendium Amoris*. We remember St John's words, 'we love because he first loved us'. This does not merely mean that having heard about God's love we are excited to love him in return: it means that the very love of God creates in us a love which is both our own and also his within us. Such is the meaning for all time of the 'tongues like flames of fire'.

Light, warmth—and burning too. The Holy Spirit will burn us. If we are to have vision, and if we are to have warmth of love, we must needs be exposed to the pain of burning. All that is fearful, unloving, selfish, hard, must be burnt out of our existence, burnt to destruction, burnt to ashes. While we think we have some Christian sight and knowledge, and while we think we have some warmth of love, there are within us unpenetrated barriers of selfishness and prejudice which resist the grace of God and thwart the light and the warmth of the Spirit. The Spirit will burn his way through to the core of our being in the ever painful process of disclosure, of penitence, and of divine forgiveness. Only by such burning can our heart be exposed fully to the warmth and our mind be exposed fully to the light. There is no seeing and no warming without burning. It is thus that we realize the saying of Jesus Christ found in one of the apocryphal documents: 'He that is near me is near the fire.'

So the Holy Spirit brings us sight, warmth, burning. He does so as the Spirit of Jesus. The seeing is a seeing through Jesus's eyes, seeing things and people less through our own spectacles of prejudice and more as Jesus sees them. The warming means the actual love that is in Jesus crucified and risen becoming our own. The burning is with the painful exposure which comes to those who find themselves in Jesus's presence. It is the Spirit of Jesus who works the work of Jesus in us. But notice, last but far from least, that in all that he does the Spirit is the Spirit of fellowship. At Pentecost the company of believers were lifted out of themselves in a common experience and were drawn into a common life. The Holy Spirit was known to them only as One in whom all shared, One who created fellowship amongst them. It is as we are drawn into fellowship with one another that the seeing and the warming and the burning of the Holy Spirit become our own. May he on this Whitsunday enable each of us in company with our fellow-Christians to see, to love, and to burn.

What is the Church?

Come to Jesus, to that living stone, rejected by men, but in God's sight chosen and precious, like living stones be yourselves built into a spiritual house.   *1 Peter 2.4*

Just nine hundred years ago Bishop Remigius, chosen after the Norman conquest to care for the vast diocese which reached from the Humber to the Thames, moved its seat from Dorchester to this lovely and strategic site on Lindum hill. It has been quaintly said of him 'he refused the tabernacle of Birinus and chose not the tribe of the South Angles, but chose the tribe of Lindsey, even the city of Lindum which he loved; and there he built his temple on high and laid the foundation of it like the ground which hath been established for ever'. Tonight[1] we remember Remigius with gratitude for his choice of this site, a choice which created the Lincoln which we know, and for the beautiful portions of his work which survive on the West Front. And we go on to recall how when Remigius's church had been devastated by an earthquake the saintly Bishop Hugh saw the beginning of its rebuilding in the loveliest Gothic, and how Bishop Grosseteste, scholar and statesman, saw the Gothic church completed, and how later still the Angel Choir was built as a home for St Hugh's shrine. When therefore we thank God today for one of the noblest works of man in stone and sculpture in this or any country, we are thanking him no less for some great Christian lives whose stories are bound up with this church.

It is very hard for us in the twentieth century to enter into the mental processes or the motives of those who designed and built our great medieval cathedrals. A love for God, most certainly, was there. So too was a devotion to the Church as an institution as powerful over men's minds and actions as any monarch or state could be. Perhaps also there was the concern for insurance about the hazards of the life-to-come, where the sombre stretches of purgatory preceded the bliss of heaven.

[1] Sermon preached in Lincoln Cathedral on the eve of St Peter's Day, 1972.

Perhaps also the motive of jealous local patriotism had its part, as 'our' church must be no less large and no less beautiful than those in other places. So with mingled motives, but with the love for God certainly powerful among them, they built this Minster. And with mingled motives it has been loved through the centuries, by some with definite and ardent Christian conviction, by some with a less defined sense of history and beauty, and by many with thoughts no more and no less than that it is *our* Minster and we love it. Yet there must be few at any period to whom this church has not at times spoken of something beyond the material boundaries of material life, something which says, 'Lift up your hearts.'

Today, however, at St Peter's festival, let St Peter himself tell us the deepest meaning of Lincoln Cathedral. Every Christian church was built because there exists this other Church of which St Peter tells. Listen to his words: 'Come to Jesus, to that living stone . . . like living stones be yourselves built up a spiritual house.' That is what the word *Church* meant to the Christians of the first century: not stone or brick or wood, but the Christian people themselves. Jesus, rejected by men and done to death on Calvary but precious in God's sight and now raised from the dead, is the corner-stone; and when men and women are converted and baptized they are united to him, and there grows, stone by stone, stone by stone, a spiritual house, Christ's home, Christ's temple, through whom Christ is now made known in the world. It is of this house of God that this Cathedral is a symbol; and of all its glories the greatest is that it is a symbol of the house made of human lives. Through the centuries this other great Church and Minster has stood: human lives united to Jesus, receiving his presence, and showing his goodness, his love, his sacrifice, his humility, his compassion. Living stones, what a mingling of metaphors! It tells of firm, solid, unmovable loyalty, and of persons alive in joy, in freedom, in creativity, in influence. This is the Church which Jesus Christ founded, the Church of which he said that the gates of death would never prevail against it.

Some searching questions are posed for all of us today. We think of the Christians of the first century. They meet in one another's houses, to pray together, to celebrate the Eucharist, to listen to the letters from an apostle, to practise fellowship in every way. Or sometimes they meet in the open air, near to some river or stream in which the converts are baptized. *They* are God's house, and they know no other. The great cathedrals are not yet. We can think too of how today there are Christians in countries of great poverty who have the simplest churches built of wood or mud, and they love them dearly and walk many miles to worship in them. Or we can think too of countries today where Christians are severely persecuted, and it is the homes of the people once again that are the meeting places of the believers. In all these ways Christians have shown, and Christians show still, that it is the people, not the buildings, that make the Church of God. There are places in this country, not least in new areas of population where this is most strikingly so.

What thoughts rise in our minds as we remember these facts?

First, we need not apologize, or regret that, when Christianity moved into the world's civilizations and cultures in order to try to bring Christ's Spirit within them, there followed the baptism of painting and music and letters and architecture into the service and praise of God, man offering to God the greatest beauty that he has to offer. Man's works, as well as Man, are claimed by God and brought to him. Hence the story of Christian art, sculpture, and architecture through the centuries, never with the Godward motive absent but always with that risk of mingled motives that belongs to Man's fallible nature.

Next, we must realize how possible it is amidst the complexities of Christian civilization to miss the simple truth of St Peter's teaching that the Church means essentially the people themselves as living stones. Not seldom have people been led to suppose that the Church means the buildings, that their upkeep is one of the primary Christian functions. Indeed, Christianity can itself appear to be identified with a particular sort of Western European culture with its chancels and naves and organs and pews and hassocks. Hence it is not surprising that, in reaction, forms of Christian fellowship are today springing up apart from the historic institutional Churches, with Christians meeting in houses, to worship and pray together, to study the Bible together, to break the bread together, feeling after the mood and the atmosphere of the first Christians. 'Experimental Christianity' as it is sometimes called, in contrast to institutional Christianity, may prove to be a growing phenomenon in our time. Indeed, it may be that the ecumenical task of the future will be less the holding together of the various older traditions, Catholic, Anglican, Protestant, than the holding together of the old institutional Churches on the one hand and the experimental types of Christianity on the other. What is certain is that exciting days for Christianity lie ahead.

Thirdly, St Peter's words challenge us about our own priorities as a Christian Church. What are the priorities in our hearts? I chanced the other day to read these words in John Ruskin's *Lectures on Art*.

> Let every dawn of morning be to you as the beginning of life, and every setting sun be to you as its close; . . . so, from day to day and from strength to strength you shall build up, by Art, by Thought and by Just Will, an *ecclesia* of England of which it shall not be said 'See what manner of stones are here' but 'See what manner of men'.

'See what manner of men.' Ruskin so rightly and characteristically saw how glorious architecture has its counterpart in lovely human lives. Perhaps a little naïvely he believed that art and letters sufficed of themselves to create Christian character, to build a Christian community. St Peter knew better. He knew about the deep estrangement of human sin. He knew, as he tells us in his First Epistle, that little gem among the books of the New Testament, how Christ bore our sins in his own body on the tree that we being dead to sin might live to righteousness, and how it was God who begat us again to a living hope by the Resurrection of Jesus Christ from the dead. He knew that such alone is the foundation of the true community of a spiritual house. Jesus is the corner-stone as being also the stone rejected in his Passion and restored in his Resurrection.

See what manner of stones are here, in this lovely Minster of Lincoln. See too what manner of men. May we before we go home today picture to ourselves what Christ's spiritual house might be, fulfilling the dreams of the old missionaries of this land. I see a community of Christians conscious of being called apart in the way of holiness, but never self-conscious as their awareness is of the God whom they worship and the people whom they serve and care for. I see such a community ardently devoted to the worship of God in a worship where awe and beauty and mystery are mingled with homeliness and fellowship. I see

such a community practising fellowship amongst themselves
as the walls of denominations yield to the discovery of unity
in Christ's truth. I see such a community marked by an intellectual integrity, open both to old truth and to new discovery,
a thoughtful faith which is, in St Peter's words, 'always ready
to give an answer to any man who asks a reason concerning
the hope that is in you'. I see such a community full of active
compassion for the poor, the homeless, the hungry, the lonely.
Such a community will influence the country as a whole with
the ideals of service not to the group or the section but to the
common good, ideals reacting far beyond our own country.
Such a community will make Christ known because its members
are living stones, Christ's own house in beauty and in lively
steadfastness. Let Lincoln Cathedral send us home today with
this vision in our hearts, and a prayer that we may serve in its
fulfilment. Let it say to us: 'They dreamed not of a perishable
home who thus could build.'

Anselm

A merciful man . . . beloved by God and men, he made him equal
to the glorious saints, and made him strong so that his enemies
feared him.   *Ecclesiasticus 45.1–3*

Dear brothers in Christ, in these words the Son of Sirach described
Moses of old, but you will see in the words a description of St
Anselm whom you in Bec and we in Canterbury love and revere.
It is for me a deep joy and privilege to join with you, the monks
of Bec, in worship and thanksgiving at the feast of the saint.[1]
May his prayers help us, as we offer our prayers and praises to
God in the communion of his saints.

How many are the aspects of St Anselm which come to our
minds. We think of him first as a man of learning and philosophy.
It was an ambition simply to acquire knowledge, a love for
letters, which brought him to Bec as a young student, sitting
at Lanfranc's feet. But he grew from the love of letters as a scholar
to the love of God as a monk, and he devoted his incomparable
powers of thought to the deepest questions about God and the
world. Unlike many of the Fathers who preceded him and many
of the Schoolmen who followed him he did not fill his books
with masses of authorities and quotations. No, he chose great
questions and reasoned about them, and perhaps because his
books are short they have been the more widely read and loved.
One great theme was constantly in his mind, the consistency of
the truth of Christian doctrine with human reason. Reason
indeed cannot create the truth, reason cannot discover it: the
order must always be *fides quaerens intellectum*. But because reason
in man is a God-given faculty, theology must be capable of
commendation to reason. And all those who through the centuries
have understood the role of reason in theology can hail St Anselm
as a guide and a father. It is in virtue of this that you revere him,
and many in our Anglican Communion revere him too and try
to learn from him still.

[1] Sermon preached in the Abbey of Bec, 20 April 1967.

Next, we think of St Anselm as monk, priest, and pastor.
Love towards God and humility in God's presence was the root of
his tenderness, sympathy, and gentleness towards those in his
spiritual care. I love the opening words of the *Proslogion*:

> Come now, little man, put aside your business for a while, take
> refuge for a little from your tumultuous thoughts; cast off
> your cares, and let your burdensome distractions wait. Take
> some leisure for God; rest awhile in him. Enter into the
> chamber of your mind; put out everything except God and
> whatever helps you to seek him; close the door and seek
> him. Say now to God with all your heart: 'I seek thy face,
> O Lord, thy face I seek.'

This spirit of single-minded devotion to God was with St
Anselm till the day of his death. And with it there went his
loving care for people. Like a great teacher he cared for his
pupils as much as for the truth, and the method of dialogue
in his writings is a symbol of the interplay of mind with mind,
of person with person, in the spirit of the proverb of Solomon,
'as in water face answereth to face, so the heart of man answereth
to man'. The love and sympathy which he showed towards his
pupils and his fellow-monks was shown no less to both friends
and enemies in the tumultuous years of his archiepiscopate.
The people of England wanted him to be their archbishop because
on his visits during Archbishop Lanfranc's reign they had found
that he loved them. The letters of St Anselm are among the
classics of pastoral writing, filled with sympathy for high and
low, rich and poor. Every reader has his favourites among the
letters. My favourite is the letter from Bec to Canterbury on
behalf of the runaway monk:

> Moses, our very dear brother, who, led astray by the unstead-
> iness of youth, forsook your cloister, has not by God's pro-
> tection wasted his substance in riotous living . . . but, without
> having exhausted the sustenance of his soul which he had
> received at your spiritual table, has at last sought refuge
> in our monastery, as in a well-known harbour.

The letter stands in the succession of the apostle Paul's letter
to Philemon.

Lastly, we cherish the name of Anselm as the heroic statesman of the Church against the intolerable claims of kings and princes. Like Moses, God 'made him strong so that his enemies stood in fear of him'. Reluctantly, unwillingly, this scholar saint found himself embroiled in statecraft and contending for the rights of the Church against kings who wanted to override those rights. By constancy and integrity he won battles without the weapons of worldly subtlety or strength. He reflects the words of the psalmist: 'Princes have persecuted me without a cause, but my heart standeth in awe of thy word.' But no tribute is finer than that of Dante in the twelfth Canto of the *Paradiso*. Describing the twelve stars in the garland of St Bonaventure, he puts Anselm happily between one who was a type of the teacher of children in the first steps of knowledge, Donatus the grammarian, and two who rebuked kings and queens in the name of truth, Nathan the prophet and John Chrysostom the preacher:

> Natan Profeta e il metropolitano
> Chrisostomo ed Anselmo e quel Donato
> che a la prim' arte degno porre mano . . .

Today we thank God for our saint, Abbot of Bec and Archbishop of Canterbury, philosopher, pastor, heroic confessor for the Church's freedom. Nothing is more attractive than the way in which amidst the tumults of statecraft he retained the mind of the student and the thinker. We remember how on his last Palm Sunday they said to him: 'Lord father, we understand that you are going to leave the world for your Lord's Easter court', and Anselm replied:

If His will be so, I shall gladly obey His will. But if He willed rather that I should yet remain amongst you, at least till I have solved a question which I am turning in my mind, about the origin of the soul, I should receive it thankfully, for I know not whether any one will finish it after I have gone.

There is perhaps a similarity in the story of the death of Richard Hooker, the great Anglican divine of the reign of Queen Elizabeth I, who also devoted himself to studying the relation of theology with human reason. Hooker, says his biographer, 'did not beg a long life of God for any other reason but to live to finish his three remaining books of Polity, and then, Lord, let thy servant depart in peace'. But he died 'meditating the order and number of angels, and their blessed obedience and order, without which peace could not be in heaven—and oh that it might be so on earth'.

On 24 March 1966, Pope Paul VI and the Archbishop of Canterbury, who both revere St Anselm greatly, signed the Common Declaration in the Church of St Paul-without-the-Walls, and in it they affirmed their desire

> that all those Christians who belong to these two Communions may be animated by these same sentiments of respect, esteem and fraternal love, and in order to help these develop to the full, they intend to inaugurate between the Roman Catholic Church and the Anglican Communion a serious dialogue which, founded on the Gospels and on the ancient common traditions, may lead to that unity in truth for which Christ prayed.

In the spirit of that declaration I bring to you, dear Father Abbot and monks of Bec, my brothers in Christ, love and greeting from Canterbury. As we join together today in gratitude to Almighty God for St Anselm we pray that God will bless greatly the monks of Bec and the Christian people of Canterbury.

May God help those who belong to the Roman Catholic Church and the Anglican Communion to grow in mutual love, in practical brotherhood, and in theological understanding. May he lead all Christians in the way of unity in holiness and in truth.

Rome and Canterbury: One Step[1]

'Null and void.' That has been the official teaching of the Church of Rome on the priesthood conferred by Anglican ordinations. The priests and the bishops in the Anglican Communion are not priests and bishops at all. An attempt to achieve a fresh view about this was made in the 1890s, and it seemed to be closed by the Bull *Apostolicae Curae* issued by Pope Leo XIII in 1896. This view about priesthood is of course congruous with the belief that the Roman Catholic Church is itself the one true Church in the world.

The conclusion of Pope Leo XIII about orders was based largely on the contention that in claiming to make men priests the Anglican Communion had a defective *intention* through not having the true belief about what priesthood means. The Anglican rejoinder was, and is, that to argue thus is to assume a concept of priesthood narrowly defined in relation to certain sixteenth-century controversies about sacrifice, and that the Anglican intention in making priests conforms to the requirements of the early centuries and to by far the greater part of the Church's history in West and East. Great prominence came to be given to this question of orders which seemed to be crucial for the relation of the Churches. It seemed that the deadlock would remain, unless one day the ground of discussion could shift.

Today's publication of an Agreed Statement on Ministry and Ordination by a group of Roman Catholic and Anglican theologians appointed respectively by the Vatican and the Archbishop of Canterbury shows that the ground has shifted. How has this happened?

It has happened because of the breakthrough which enables scholars of the two Communions, with official encouragement,

[1] From *The Guardian*, December 1973, on the day of the publication of the document *Ministry and Ordination* by the Anglican–Roman Catholic International Commission, under the joint chairmanship of the Roman Catholic Bishop of Elmham, the Rt Rev. Alan Clark and the Anglican Bishop of Ossory, the Rt Rev. Henry McAdoo.

to discuss the issues not separately but *together*. This in itself is an immense step forward when one recalls the climate of fairly recent times. At my meeting with Pope Paul VI on 24 March 1966 he and I signed together the 'Common Declaration' in which we were pledged 'to inaugurate between the Roman Catholic Church and the Anglican Communion a serious dialogue which, founded on the Gospels and the ancient common traditions, may lead to that unity in truth for which Christ prayed'. This hope was fulfilled not only by considerable informal dialogue in many countries but by the officially appointed Joint Commission which produced the Statement on the Eucharist at the end of 1971 and now the Statement on the Ministry.

The Statement does not discuss what orders are or are not valid. It does not directly tackle the Roman–Anglican controversy. But, like the Statement on the Eucharist, it goes behind the post-sixteenth-century controversies and, using the scriptures and the early traditions as a guide, it asks: What is the essence of priesthood? What does it mean to be a priest? It answers those questions in relation to the unique priesthood of Christ, the priesthood of all Christians in the Church and, in that context, the special priesthood of the ordained ministry. What is a priest? What does he exist to do? What does his ordination mean? These basic questions are answered, and answered unanimously, by the widely drawn group of Roman Catholic and Anglican divines.

What authority has the document? Only the authority of its authors. What is it likely to achieve? I believe it is likely to encourage and extend the trend in both Churches to go behind the later controversies and to recover the primitive concepts. And I cannot but think that this process, as it grows in the thinking of Roman Catholics and Anglicans, will before too long affect the influence of the Bull of Pope Leo XIII. For if priesthood is understood to be what the learned Roman Catholic, as well as Anglican, authors of the document say it is, then Pope Leo XIII will seem less right or wrong than irrelevant. Let that, however, be said in humility rather than in any 'I told you so' spirit, for we may all one day wake up to the painful irrelevance of some of our polemical positions.

There are other formidable questions still to be tackled, and these will not be underrated. The way to unity is not the way of indifferentism, but—as in the question of orders—the way of a deeper understanding of truth. Greater agreement is needed for the unrestricted intercommunion for which we long, for if there is doubt as to whether another Christian body is part of the true Church and whether its priests are real priests, communion is bound to be hindered. Today's document brings the day of reconciliation nearer.

Unity: Why and Wherefore?

Called to be saints together with all those who in every place call
on the name of our Lord Jesus Christ.   *1 Corinthians 1.2*

It is a moving experience for me to be welcomed tonight in the
City Temple.[1] It is just fifty-two years since a sensation was caused
when a leading Anglican clergyman preached in the City Temple.
It was Dr Hensley Henson, at the time Dean of Durham, and his
coming here was regarded as a very controversial event. The Bishop
of London of the time strongly deprecated the visit and wrote
that if Dr Henson wished to address the people of the City Temple
he should do so in some 'neutral hall'. 'Neutral hall': you have
only to repeat that phrase to realize how immense has been the
change. And in the change no part has been more significant
than the shedding of the old self-consciousness. Tonight we
meet in the unselfconscious happiness of Christian brotherhood.
And I know of no words which define and justify this so well
as the words of the apostle when he describes the Christian
community in Corinth, and by implication any and every
Christian community in the world, as 'called to be saints together
with all who in every place call on the name of our Lord Jesus
Christ'.

What words those are! How they lift us out of our limitations
into the supreme facts. You, as lay people or ministers in your
own Churches, and I as a chief pastor in mine, are one. And we
are one not because of our own ability to grasp things (indeed
we grasp things very little), still less because of any virtues we may
be supposed to have, but because Christ has called us and we
accept his call. When we say Christ called us we are at once in
his hands, we are held by him, for him to do with us what he
intends to do. And what he intends our text goes on to say.
We are called—*to be saints*, called to resemble Jesus, called to be
moulded into the likeness of Jesus crucified. That is what
Christianity is about. 'Called to be saints', says St Paul; 'we shall

[1] On Sunday, 11 January 1969.

be like him, for we shall see him as he is', says St John. And,
if that is what Christianity is about, it is no less what Christian
unity is about. And the picture in our text moves on, inevitably,
inexorably: called, called to be saints, with all who in every place
call on the name of Jesus. For to have this calling, however poorly
we understand it, and to have this goal, however miserably we
fall short of it, is to be one with anyone else, with everyone else
who has this same call and this same goal. 'All who in every place
call on the name of Jesus.' Are there people tonight calling on
the name of Jesus in the City Temple, in St Paul's Cathedral,
in Westminster Cathedral, in Spurgeon's Tabernacle, in the
Orthodox Greek Cathedral, in the silent meeting of the Quakers,
in houses where two or three Christians are praying together?
Here indeed is a unity not made by us, not chosen by us, but
created by Christ, from whose call we cannot escape. He is stronger
than we, and he has prevailed.

Now to rejoice in this basic unity, whether we think of it as
the unity of faith or as the unity of the baptized (the apostles knew
no distinction between those two aspects), to rejoice in this
basic unity is not to deny but rather to emphasize the need for
this unity to have right expression in creed, in sacraments, in
ordered church fellowship. Christ who called us gave to us of his
goodness the revelation of God's truth, sacraments to unite us to
himself and to one another, ministers to speak in his name.
Here is part of our ecumenical task, to recover the right ordered
expression of that unity which Christ has given to us. In this
recovery we can thank God for the wonderful advances of recent
years, and we can look with hope at much which is happening
today. I could speak tonight of some of those hopes. I could speak
of the plans for the union of Congregationalists and Presbyterians
in this country, ardently hoping that these plans may succeed. I
could speak of the plans for the union of Anglicans and Methodists
in this country, ardently hoping that these plans too may succeed.
And in no way inconsistent with these longings is my equal longing that the new understanding between Roman Catholics and
other Christians may deepen and widen as we discover ourselves
not as rivals but as brothers and allies within Christendom. I use
the word Christendom deliberately, and by it I do not mean a
whole Christian civilization, for alas, a whole Christian civilization is today far to seek! I mean rather the fact that Christians in

the world are despite their divisions a single phenomenon, a community who share so much that their united impact could even now be very great. See ourselves as those who in every place are called to be saints, and we are indeed a corporate entity, the Christians. An old writer said: 'As the soul is in the body so are Christians in the world.' It is of this role of Christians in the world that I now speak.

The faith to which we are called is a faith which knows where it stands in relation to the claims of contemporary scientific humanism. Scientific humanism stands for a reverence for man and a concern for his dignity, freedom, and happiness, together with the belief that the advance of the sciences and the application of scientific methods will make the human race more efficient, more happy, and also more moral. And scientific humanism looks for the disappearance of religion as it holds that religion opposes the scientific spirit and diverts people from their intelligent service of their fellows by false otherworldly preoccupations. We must share the humanists' reverence for man. We can acknowledge that bad religion can be anti-scientific and can promote the wrong kind of otherworldliness. But we challenge the sufficiency of the humanist diagnosis of man's troubles and the humanist view of the answer to them. For immense advances in science and knowledge can leave man proud and selfish and cruel, and the desperate need is not just for more knowledge and more progress (good though these things are and demanding our concern) but for the putting right of a radical estrangement between man and his Creator: 'He hath shewed thee, O man, what is good; and what doth the Lord thy God require of thee, but to do justly and to love mercy and to walk humbly with thy God?' We renew the prophet's question, and we proclaim the answer, which Bethlehem gives, an answer which St Augustine summed up in these words: 'So deep has human pride sunk us that only divine humility can raise us.'

It is, however, in no facile way that we can dare to affirm this faith. It is a costly faith to which we are called, and never more so than at this time, a costly faith with the Cross at its centre. It is terribly hard for so many thoughtful people to think that the universe, so bewildering and so seemingly chaotic and capricious, has within it or beyond it a purpose, a meaning, a direction, a sovereign power. As Christians we dare to say that it

has, only in terms of the death and resurrection of Jesus. Only
in terms of living through dying, of losing self so as to find self,
of sacrificial love, can we say there is a sovereign power at work,
and so our affirmation of Christian theism goes hand in hand with
our readiness for the way of the Cross. If as a Christian community
in the world we had a faith like that and lived as if we believed it,
what a difference this would make to the credibility of our
message. St Paul knew his faith and his Christian calling as 'always
bearing about in the body the dying of Jesus, that the life also
of Jesus may be manifested in our body'.

Again, we are called as Christians to a faith which both cares
intensely about this world and is also set upon another world
beyond it. The first is an immediate test of our Christianity. Men
and women, and specially the younger men and women of our
time, just will not listen to us unless our faith is filled with a practical caring for our fellows. Our concern in action for the hungry
and the homeless, for right dealing between different races, for
the laws of conduct which God has given us, shows whether we
love God whom we have not seen by the test of our love for the
brother we have seen. But as we serve this world and its needs we
are all the while laying hold of something beyond this world,
an eternal life which gives this world its true perspective. Let
not that be forgotten. We are here not only to do things, we are
here to be something, to become something—and that is the meaning of our being called to be saints. Christianity is about our
doing things here, and about our being something whose goal
is beyond here. The Christians are in the world as the soul is in
the body by keeping alive for themselves and for others the hope
of heaven, where (in Thomas Binney's words which I am sure
you sometimes sing):

> The sons of ignorance and night
> shall dwell in the eternal light
> through the eternal love.

Called—called to be saints—with all that in every place call
upon the name of Jesus: that is what the week of prayer for Christian unity is about. It is this calling and this hope which create
for us our present oneness, making us the Christians in the world.
And while we pray for the horizontal realization of unity in the
drawing closer together, in whatever way Christ designs, of

Anglicans, Free Churchmen, Roman Catholics, and all of us, making the one nearer to the other, we also pray for that other dimension—call it vertical if you like, words are inadequate—that other dimension of nearness to Jesus in the working out within each of us of the calling to be saints. May he who humbled himself in the stable in Bethlehem and on the wood on the mound of Cavalry so humble us that something of his likeness may begin to be ours. To this he has called us, and has made us one with all in every place who have the same call and dare not look back.

Anglicans and Methodists

This speech was made in the General Synod of the Church of England on 3 May 1972 in proposing a motion to approve the two-stage scheme for union between the Church of England and the Methodist Church. The Methodist Church had already endorsed the scheme. It had been agreed that a 75 per cent vote was required for giving authority to the decision, and at the end of the debate the majority was insufficient—the voting being

bishops	for	34	against	6
clergy	for	152	against	80
laity	for	117	against	87

I am told that if this resolution passes with sufficient authority it will be a miracle. I pray for this miracle, but miracles can be very frightening. And I should be very frightened of this miracle happening, unless there is to be another miracle for which we all can pray together: that whether today we say 'Yes' or 'No', we may all be given a mutual forbearance, a humility before God of a frankly 'beyond-this-world' kind. And in that humility we may know more than ever that our little earthen vessels with our so-called successes or so-called failures are not what makes the Church of God. Come what may, Christ the Lord of the Church reigns, and something which may loom very large at any moment in our consciousness is a tiny little incident in Christ's empire in human lives which is what the Church means.

The question is before us today, awaiting our 'Yes' or our 'No', because the Methodist Church has posed the question to us and is eager to hear our answer, and will be listening to us throughout our discussions. That the Methodist Church has given its own answer 'Yes' and is awaiting ours is itself a remarkable event in history. If half a century ago this possibility had been forecast it would have sounded quite remarkable; and it would have sounded yet more remarkable if it had been forecast that a Methodist 'Yes' would be followed by a Church of England 'No'.

If, however, there are compelling reasons for saying 'No',

then we must say 'No'. I think my best way of starting today's discussion, which is all I intend to do, is to look at some of the reasons for saying 'No'.

1. First, and I think this is for some the matter of most concern to them: the contention that the Service of Reconciliation is doctrinally unsound.

Now some are worried by the fact that whereas those who have received the rite of unification in North India are acceptable by us as priests without any change in our Canon, in the case of Methodist ministers who received the Service of Reconciliation a change in the Canon would be needed. This is represented as altering the doctrine of the Church of England. The difference is, however, solely one of legal technicality because the Canon was framed to refer to those ordained in another Church. There would be no difference doctrinally in the status of North India presbyters and presbyters who received the Anglican–Methodist Reconciliation. What I am saying is the view expressed clearly by the Dean of the Arches.

If there is a doctrinal difference between the effects of the two services let us be shown it from the text of the services themselves. Compare what happens in the two services, that is what matters. In neither case is the service described as an ordination, nor is it likely that the recipients would describe themselves as being ordained. In both services God is asked, in answer to prayer with the laying on of hands, to give what he knows the recipient to need for the office of presbyter in the Church of God. Both rites include a declaration of willingness to accept what God wills to give. In virtue of this both rites include the essence of what conditional ordination means. Comparing the two we see that the Anglican–Methodist rite uses more explicit language about the priestly functions of the office for which the gift is given.

If this Synod really proposes to tell the rest of Christendom that whereas the North India rite is sound doctrine and assured in what it asked God to give, the Anglican–Methodist service is unsound doctrine and even immoral, I don't think the rest of Christendom is going to find this Synod credible. Indeed, I would go further. Theology is about God. What sort of God is it who was willing and able to answer the prayer with laying on of hands in the North India scheme and is not willing or able to answer the prayer in the Anglican–Methodist service?

I understand the feelings of the Evangelicals, some of them, who say that having two different layings on of hands for the Anglicans and for the Methodists implies the making of a query about Methodist orders. But the Methodist Church has said it is willing to accept this and wants us to accept it too.

2. There has been the contention that if we say 'Yes' today we shall be damaging the prospects of growing understanding between the Anglican Communion and the Church of Rome.

At present, as we know, the Church of Rome officially regards our orders as null and void, and the shadow of Pope Leo XIII's Bull of 1896 still hovers over the scene. But new understandings are on the way. The recently published Agreed Statement on the Eucharist produced by the Anglican–Roman Catholic International Commission is a notable instance of new understanding. Now will the proposals before the Synod today hinder this process of growing understanding?

It is not the view either of the Anglican or of the Roman Catholic Chairman of the International Commission that they will. Of course varieties of view exist amongst Roman Catholics, but it is a mistake to overlook very weighty views which are sympathetic. I refer to an article by Bishop Alan Clark in the *Catholic Herald* for 18 February. Here the Bishop expresses concern about one point, the continuing relations with non-episcopal Churches, but he counsels patience about this and says: 'It would not be inhuman to ask us to remember the time factor, the two stages in the reunion, and not to condemn too precipitately.' On the Service of Reconciliation, so far from being outraged by it, Bishop Clark writes: 'A careful reading of the document shows that, though the language is different from ours, it provides for a prayer to God that any defect in ministry may by his power be remedied. A Catholic theologian might well call this conditional ordination.' At the end of the article Bishop Clark writes: 'We are intensely interested in the whole courageous enterprise, and sensitive to the issues at stake. Whatever the outcome we can only be grateful that the attempt was made, and in all this we reverence the presence of the Spirit of God.'

No less interesting is the article by Bishop Christopher Butler in *The Tablet* of 9 January. He writes enthusiastically about the Anglican–Methodist Ordinal; and when he comes on to the Service of Reconciliation, so far from regarding it as a disaster, he poses the question whether, if it includes the essence of conditional ordination, it may not be the method eventually employed in the solution of Anglican–Roman Catholic relations. I would myself be very hesitant about this idea; but it would not be surprising if the concept of the Service of Reconciliation were to come constructively within the field of Anglican–Roman Catholic discussions.

In fairness I mention one caveat which Bishop Butler makes in the same article. He expresses anxiety to be sure that the Scheme is to be interpreted by the Ordinal. It is not for me to make pronouncements about how the Scheme is to be interpreted. So I will only say that when both Churches adopt an Ordinal for invariable use, inevitably that Ordinal will express what each Church means by Holy Orders.

3. Now for another contention: that if these proposals were once for all put out of the way it would be easier to advance in one stage towards a united Church with the Methodists and perhaps with others.

It is said that if we were starting now we would be going straight for a one-stage united Church. That may be so: I don't know that it is so, but it may be so. But we are not starting now, and we never are starting now. We and the Methodists have together moved along the present path through a series of decisions made in favour of a two-stage scheme; and it was at the behest of us Anglicans that the two stages were desired. Our Church has committed itself to its desire for union in two stages in overwhelming votes in 1969. Now are we to say to the Methodists: 'You accepted what was after all our own proposal in principle; but now would you mind considering something else instead'?

And are we sure that agreement amongst ourselves would be more easily forthcoming for the kind of united Church that might be devised? My own postbag, a very considerable one, tells me that a large part of the opposition among us is opposition to going into a united Church and losing our own Church's separate identity.

We have to face the difference between moving to a united Church in a country such as India and moving to a united Church in this country. In India Christian Churches travel light, with missionary mobility and without the heavy weight of ecclesiastical history and the deep roots of cultural traditions. Here in England we have the heavy weights of ecclesiastical history and organization and the deep roots of cultural tradition. These things make any move towards a united Church difficult. Something needs to happen. Somehow there must be a breakthrough. Something must happen. Just now two things have happened. One is the actual union of the Presbyterians and the Congregationalists. The other is the decision of the Methodists already to accept the proposals we are discussing as a decisive step towards a united Church. A breakthrough has happened. I don't think we are going to be nearer to a united Church if this Synod says 'No' today.

4. Then there is a totally different kind of plea that the ecumenical cause would advance better if we said 'No' today. It is the plea that the ecumenical movement is moving into a new phase in which structural schemes between Churches are out of date.

Now let me say that I have very much sympathy with this plea. I believe myself that we are learning that the heart of ecumenism is renewal, that we need to dwell far less upon our ecclesiastical structures and far more upon what we can do together as Christians, learning from one another across the denominational borders, in the deepening of spirituality, in the exploring of theological depth, in evangelism together, and in together saying something and doing something towards the secular community beyond the Church's frontier. I gave voice myself to something of this in the little book which I wrote jointly with Cardinal Suenens called *The Future of the Christian Church*. If we pursue this path it may be that in time free local developments will alter the total scene and one day make structural union inevitable. It may also be that the problem of intercommunion should be tackled not on the basis of relationships between Churches but on the basis that intercommunion may happen locally, with the guidance of the bishop, where local fellowship is deep and genuine.

But, now, will all this be helped if the Synod says 'No' today? I find it hard to believe that it will. We have existing obligations to the Methodists, our very near spiritual kindred, having led

Hc

them up the present path. And again and again it is reported from the localities that while something can be done about inter-communion, deep and effective fellowship is hampered by the problem of *ministries*. So I believe that to say 'Yes' to Stage 1 will not hinder, but help, that trend of renewal, of a more free and outreaching ecumenism, for which the plea is so rightly being made.

Where are we now? If we say 'No' today, what shall we be saying to the Methodists? 'Dear Methodists, the General Synod says "No" to you, because it is so keen to have a united Church with you and others in a better way than this scheme allows', or 'Dear Methodists, the General Synod says "No" to you because it doesn't want any schemes at all.' I hope we shall say neither.

5. This brings me to the last contention I want to discuss: the contention that the scheme is so divisive.

We are accepting scrupulously the proviso that a majority of 75 per cent is needed for an answer 'Yes'. Within that proviso we vote in accord with our own judgement and conscience. We weigh up the fact that there is within the Church a great deal of dislike for these proposals. But I hope we do this weighing up with a sense of history in our minds. History! I recall a series of episodes in the history of our Church when there has been formidable opposition to something or other, not least amongst the clergy. Doom had been predicted. But the thing happened. Doom never came. But a new perspective came in which what had seemed dreadful proved not to be dreadful at all. The last of such episodes was just thirty years ago when some formidable people in the Church told Archbishop Temple that if the South India Scheme went forward with the approval of the Anglican Communion there might be a secession; and later it was said that two thousand priests would be affected by it. Archbishop Temple did not lose his nerve at this, perhaps because he knew that his own father had faced the same kind of thing and had not lost his nerve. Of the two thousand I know of three who went to Rome. I know of a good many of the two thousand who are happily with us, and I know of some who are now recommending the Church of South India Order as the right solution for us today. But today the situation is different. The many people who in different synods have opposed these proposals are not one united body of threatening non-jurors. They are people of many different sorts. Some don't like the scheme because it fails to be Catholic. Others don't like it because it is too Catholic. Some don't like it because they want more freedom for the Spirit. Others don't like it, and they are very many, because they don't like change at all. We must not assume of other people, which we never assume about ourselves, that when they don't like something and vote against it, it means they walk out.

So each of us follows his own conscience and forms his own judgement. My prayer has been that by saying 'Yes' the Synod will say to the Methodists, our brothers in faith and our cousins in church history, 'Yes. You said you would go with us in this way. And we now say Yes, we will go with you.'

Whither Christian Unity?

The occasion of this lecture[1] is the inauguration in Jesus Lane of the federation of two Anglican colleges, Westcott House and Ridley Hall, and one Methodist college, Wesley House, in the work of the training of ordained ministers, an event which is hailed with gratitude in Cambridge and far beyond. It happens at a time when those who care about Christian unity have been finding both joys and griefs in plenty. Among the joys is the jubilee of the Church of South India, which was celebrated last month, and the inauguration just a fortnight ago of the United Reformed Church formed of Presbyterians and Congregationalists in England and Wales. There are also the happy trends apparent in the relations between the Church of Rome and the Anglican Communion. As illustrations of this we have the Agreed Statement on the Eucharist produced by the Anglican–Roman Catholic International Commission and the recent lecture by Cardinal Willebrands in the library at Lambeth Palace when he reaffirmed very clearly the ideal of 'union without absorption', an ideal which had seemed revolutionary when it was put forward by the late Dom Beauduin in the Malines Conversations with the title 'L'Église Anglaise unie non absorbée'. But when I turn to the griefs I think of the blunder, as I see it, of the Synod of my own Church concerning Anglican–Methodist union on 3 May this year. If old friends in Cambridge ask what I think of this I might be tempted to reply in the words of Aeneas to Dido: 'infandum, regina, iubes renovare dolorem'.

When I was present on 4 October (1972) as a guest at the inauguration of the United Reformed Church I ventured to use these words: 'None of us wants uniformity or believes that uniformity is possible or desirable, but I am sure there is amongst us a growing conviction that somehow the heirs of the Prayer Book, the heirs of the Ejectment, and the people called Methodists are meant to be one Church.' I was not a little moved when that remark evoked from the large assembly of English Dissenters

[1] Delivered in Cambridge, 21 October 1972.

more enthusiastic assent than any remark I can remember making. History will not fail to note the growth amongst English Non-conformity in recent years of the belief that a federation is not enough and that the Christians in each place ought to be one single Christian fellowship. We Anglicans have said this in the past, but have shrunk from the cost of what it means. No doubt an initiative may come from the United Reformed Church for the reopening of a move towards a united Church in this country, and I cannot doubt that within the Church of England there will be the desire to respond to this. If this happens I hope we shall be ready to face the consequential issues of Church and State which are involved. I am sure there can be no united Church in this country without a considerable alteration in the form of the Church–State connection. It is inconceivable that Free Churchmen would join in a united Church which did not choose its own chief pastors, and if we Anglicans are serious about unity we shall not delay in facing this issue.

Meanwhile the emphasis is rightly upon *local* developments of unity, and I cannot doubt that lack of local partnership and mutual knowledge was a factor against the success of the Anglican–Methodist proposals. Local partnership in cities, towns, villages, and not least in the new areas of population, is the neces-sary context for any major union to happen. In this process we may find not a little which is frustrating and confusing unless steps are taken towards union with a more than local authority.

My purpose this evening is, however, not to discuss schemes but to consider with you some of the trends which are apparent in the ecumenical scene.

I take first the theme which is now popularly called Renewal. We notice the shift from the hope of uniting the Churches much as they are now to the hope that by the altering of them in the renewal of their life they may find union both possible and significant. When we read today the earlier literature of the ecumenical movement we find a strangely complacent assumption that the various structures have in their present state virtues so palpable that a wider Church or a theological synthesis could mean, to put it crudely, 'more of the sort of thing we have already'. Nothing did more to shift the priority from union as such to renewal than the influence of Pope John XXIII through the Second Vatican Council. Inspired by the prayer of our Lord, 'that they may all be one', Pope John saw, as the seventeenth chapter of St John indeed teaches, that if all are to become one they must become different through a closer union with Christ; and starting at home Pope John insisted that the Roman Catholic Church must be re-formed in its interior life and in the functioning of its worship, its fellowship, and its mission. Whether *propter hoc* or *post hoc* in relation to Pope John, Christians in every tradition are now found asking first of all, not: how may we unite our structures with those of other Churches? but, how may the Holy Spirit of Christ re-form our structures and ourselves for the better serving of Christ? and, what may we learn from one another in the process? It is then discovered that Churches, struggling with their own renewal, are often asking the same questions and finding many of the same answers.

So renewal has become the paramount theme. Yet it has not happened that renewal and reunion always walk in easy harmony together. This is because renewal involves divine judgement, and divine judgement is never comfortable. So it happens that Churches, praying for renewal and exposing themselves to the divine judgement, find that the forces of spiritual renewal are often at work beyond their own structures as well as within them.

So the next trend which is very conspicuous is the spread of Christian revivals of a non-institutional and experimental kind. These take a variety of forms. There are the Pentecostal revivals, partly within the historic Churches but mainly outside them. There is the movement known as the Jesus Kids, with their ardent devotion and fellowship and with the power of influencing lives in the world of drug culture. There are also those, drawn partly from the historic Churches, who prefer Christian fellowship in experimental groups, meeting in homes or places of work for worship, sacrament, study, and the planning of Christian social action. Harvey Cox in his book *The Secular City* predicted that the real ecumenical task of the future would be not the uniting of Catholic and Protestant but the holding together of institutional and experimental forms of Christianity. In his more recent book *The Feast of Fools* he notes that some of the experimental movements dwell upon mysticism and religious celebration and others of them dwell upon social activism, and he characterizes the two respectively as the new mystics and the new militants. He adds: 'Just as Catholics and Protestants need one another

in the Church, so the celebrators of life and the seekers of justice
need one another in the world. They all belong together.'

'They all belong together.' Thus complex is our ecumenical
scene today. There are the historic Churches, more than ever
involved with one another, more than ever discovering a common
Christian consciousness, yet hampered by the weight of their
institutional past and looking for renewal to deliver them into a
better service of Christ and a breakthrough towards union. Yet
renewal includes the challenges of experimental Christianity,
and not a few younger Christians would dismiss both history and
form and be impatient of any interest in church structures whether
they be separate or uniting. It is a scene with much muddle and
confusion. But it is a scene in which the Spirit of Christ, the Spirit
of love and power and indeed of Truth, is mightily present. We
may be bewildered, but we need not be afraid.

In this situation we need, and this is the third theme I would
dwell upon, some new appraisal of the relation between the Spirit
and the historic Church.

In seeking a new appraisal we turn to the New Testament
writings, and there we find a kind of double polarity between
the historical given-ness of the Church on the one hand and the
receiving of the creative energies of the Holy Spirit on the other.
The Messiah implies the messianic community, and from an
Israel which was rejecting him Jesus gathered a remnant to be
the nucleus of the new Israel, trained them to be his people,
and with them made a new covenant in his death. The new *ecclesia*
lived under the continuing rule of the risen Jesus and was in-
dwelt by his Spirit, its members called to be saints. In order to be
faithful to his lordship the Church needed both a tradition of
rite and teaching which witnessed to Christ's words and actions
in history, and also an openness to the actions of the Holy Spirit
in particular situations, challenging, interpreting, commanding.
Those two aspects of the Church may be called the horizontal
and the vertical, and both are necessary. If it relied upon the vertical actions of the Holy Spirit alone the Church might be misled
through forgetting the total stream of Christian community
through the centuries and the authority of the tradition of Christ
in history. But if it relied upon the horizontal tradition alone the
Church could let its hold upon basic truth become fossilized
through missing the Spirit's challenges to new perceptions and

new actions. It is not difficult to trace in history the salutary interplay of those factors, and the harm which follows the neglect of
one or other of them.

The tradition is indeed God-given and Christ-made, and it
is not for the Church to abandon the scriptures, the sacraments,
and the apostolic ministry. In the first book which I ever wrote,
when I was a very young man, *The Gospel and the Catholic Church*,
I advanced the thesis that the Church's visible order in ministry
and sacrament is the expression of the gospel in its historical
given-ness, and that by the dying-to-itself of the members in
union with one another and with Christ the structure of the Church
witnesses to Christ's death and resurrection. 'The structure of
Catholicism', I wrote, 'is the expression of the Gospel.' If you ask
today whether I still adhere to this youthful thesis my answer is:
'Yes, I still adhere to it'; but I would not press the metaphor of
structure in the same way, for the language of structure is but one
amongst the metaphors for the Church, and all the metaphors
need to be seen together: building, body, vine, *ecclesia*. Each
of the metaphors speaks of the one-for-all given-ness of the
Church and each of them speaks also of the growth of the Church
in its way to becoming perfectly what it is. Into the metaphor
of the temple, for instance, there bursts another metaphor,
for the stones of the temple are *living* stones. The sacramental
order of the Church witnesses to its historical given-ness, and
(as I now realize more than I once did) also witnesses to its growth
towards a plenitude when the Church, partly within history and
partly beyond history, will become its own true self.

Now when the historical aspect of the Church is balanced
by a new emphasis upon the futuristic or eschatological aspect
we begin to get light upon our problem of the relation of the
historic Church and the experimental movements. In a striking
essay in his book *Chrétiens en Dialogue*,[1] Father Yves Congar has
argued that the concept of the Church as once for all created and
as also growing towards a future plenitude can help in the combining of a Catholic ecclesiology with a recognition of the positive
significance of communities outside the Catholic Church. He was
of course dealing with the particular problem of Roman Catholic
ecclesiology *vis-à-vis* non-Roman Catholic Christianity. He
suggested that movements outside the historic institution may

[1] E.T., *Dialogue between Christians*. London 1966.

help to correct the institution's failings and may thus contribute to the Church's own growth into the full understanding of itself. He went on to depict the final unity of the Church not as a process of 'coming back to Mother' but as the converging of all Christians upon a goal which will be a Church different from any now visible yet in continuity of identity with the Church as once founded.

The influence of this line of thought was apparent within the Vatican Council in statements combining a Roman Catholic ecclesiology with a new realism about the Church of Rome itself and a new recognition of the positive significance of other types of Christianity for the Roman Catholic Church itself. Perhaps this line of thought may help all of us who in different contexts have to wrestle with our adherence to the given-ness of the Church and its sacramental order and our sensitivity to contemporary spiritual movements. We cherish the gift of historic faith and order not as the walls of an enclosed fortress but as gifts of God which both witness to the past and serve the building of a future as yet unrealized. By thus combining the historical and the futur-istic notes in our understanding of the Church we may be helped in our efforts to combine a loyalty to tradition with a sensitivity to contemporary movements. If this is a difficult adventure it is not one which need endanger our souls. Rather might our souls be endangered if we were content either to rest in past tradition undisturbed or to share in contemporary enthusiasms without relation to the stream of Christian witness through the ages.

There is one more trend which I would ask you to consider. It is the trend summarized in the phrase 'the Church for the world', the belief that we understand the Church not by concentrating upon it as a thing in itself but by looking beyond the Church to the world which it exists to serve and to re-create.

To illustrate this theme I would quote from a World Council of Churches publication, *The Church for Others*:

> The Church exists for the world . . . the Church lives in order that the world may know its own true being. It is *pars pro toto*. It is the first fruits of the new creation . . . its centre lies outside itself; it must live 'excentrally'. It has to seek out those situations in the world which call for loving responsibility, and there it must convince and point to *shalom*.[1]

[1] *The Church for Others* (WCC, Geneva; 4e., 1969), p. 18.

The same thesis is found in the writings of the Roman Catholic theologian Hans Urs von Balthasar. In his book *A Theology of History* he argues that the Church is the servant of God's purpose in and for history, and for that reason must not look for history to be drawn into itself. The Church, he says, is sent into the world to be itself a picture of the world becoming re-created after God's will. In other words it should not be the Church's preoccupation to lead people to participate in its religious activities so much as to enter human situations and make some of them more Christlike.[1]

Parallel to this concept of the Church's mission there has been the upsurging of Christian social activism within the ecumenical movement in the past decade. This was notably apparent at the Assembly of the World Council of Churches at Uppsala in 1968, with the concern about race, poverty, pollution, and the Third World. But it would be a mistake to see only a kind of modern social gospel in this phase. It goes deeper. Indeed, the concept of the Church for the world is akin to the ancient Greek theology which taught that through the existence of the Church as the body of the risen Jesus Christ the world itself begins to be re-created. Dr Nicolas Zernov thus summarizes a body of patristic teaching on this theme.

> The East does not think about salvation in terms of the individual soul returning to its maker; it is visualized, rather, as a gradual process of transfiguration of the cosmos culminating in theosis or the deification in Christ of the members of the Church as representatives and spokesmen of the creation. Man is saved not from the world but with the world because he is its guardian and master.[2]

Immense issues, and difficult ones, here face the contemporary Church. It is more and more apparent that Christians are incredible unless they stand with the underprivileged in the world, and that the Church is incredible if it is not clearly on the side of justice in the world's conflicts. This is behind the powerful swing towards Christian social and political activism, and I have mentioned the deep theological root which such an activism can have. Yet the Church is called to resist the temptation to

---

[1] Balthasar, *A Theology of History* (London 1963), pp. 132ff.
[2] N. Zernov, *The Church of the Eastern Christians* (London 1942), p. 54.

justify itself by its political and social works, remembering how the Messiah resisted a like temptation in the wilderness when he said No to the idea of using either Bread or Power to win the world to God. Thus the Church's energies for the world's re-creation are to be rooted in the Church's message of reconciliation to God, and the Church's power of being the soul of the world is linked with its otherworldly calling, witnessing to heaven as man's true home. No two Christian teachers combined a down-to-earth passion for humanity with an otherworldliness more vividly than John Chrysostom in Constantinople and John Wesley throughout England. Let Orthodox and Methodist wisdom combine to show us the otherworldly roots of the world's re-creation.

Those are some of the trends in the ecumenical scene around us. There is the quest of renewal, into which there break experimental movements which both excite renewal and complicate it. There is the conviction that Churches should unite, sometimes cut across by a sceptical apathy about Churches altogether. There is the plea that the Church should forget itself in serving the world in its distress. There is the call for a new appraisal of the doctrine of Christ, the Spirit, and the Church. So if we like things to be tidy we shall be very discouraged. But we shall not be discouraged if we see that all of these trends are within the life of the people of Christ, and within all of them the Spirit of Christ is blowing powerfully. We are being challenged on all sides both to practical Christian obedience and to theological seriousness. Here in Cambridge the tasks before the new federation of Colleges are tasks theological through and through. And the names of Ridley and Westcott and Wesley will stand to remind us that theology is nothing apart from the true liberation of mankind and the call to holiness with the vision of God as its goal.

Europe and the Faith

The happiness which my visit to Lyons[1] gives me is enhanced by two historical circumstances. One is that it happens during the Week of Prayer for Christian Unity which is being observed at this time by thousands of Christians in France, in England, and in many countries. This observance owes its inception to the initiative of the Abbé Couturier who was specially known and loved here in Lyons. He saw that if Christians of separated Churches and traditions are to be drawn into the unity for which Jesus Christ prayed, they must not only work together and study together and plan together, but they must first of all pray together. To the Abbé Couturier Christendom owes a great debt, for it is through his influence that many Christians in many countries are bound together in a brotherhood of mutual prayer. It is from the spiritual root of united prayer that one day all Christians will find the fruition of the unity which is the will of Christ for all his disciples in the world.

The other event to which I refer is the entry of Great Britain into the European Economic Community. As the linking together of countries on the Continent becomes closer and as Britain is drawn nearer to them, our thoughts are focused upon Europe both as a fact and as a concept. What kind of Europe will the Europe of the future be?

Here in Lyons one is conscious of the historic links between Europe and Christianity. It is moving to recall the ancient city of Lugdunum where several of the Roman Emperors lived for a time and where a famous group of Christians gave their lives as martyrs; and history travels on to the medieval city where several Popes had their home and where two important Councils of the Church were held. It is therefore fair to describe Lyons as a symbol of the making of Europe, for Europe was created by the impact of Christianity upon the nations which swept into the territories in the declining years of the Roman Empire. Europe was a reality. Despite the differences between the often

[1] Lecture given on 22 January 1973.

warring nationalities within it, it possessed a spiritual unity, and of this spiritual unity the Romanesque and Gothic cathedrals and churches still stand as a visible sign. There was the common belief that Man has a divine Creator to whom he is responsible and a destiny beyond this world, and of this belief the *Divina Commedia* of Dante is the lasting literary legacy.

Today the old Europe is but faintly visible. Its cathedrals stand, its literature is still read—by some, its saints are revered, and its faith is still practised by thousands. But no longer is the Christian faith the dominant force in the lives and the morals of the people. It would take long to describe the break-up of the old Catholic Europe, with its synthesis in thought and its unity in faith and culture; and indeed no two historians would describe the process in the same way. There was the revolt against the corruptions of ecclesiastical power in the Middle Ages. There were the religious divisions of the Reformation period. There was the force of nationalism, sometimes mixed up with the religious divisions. There was the rise of the modern sciences and of a scientific outlook not always easy to reconcile with the outlook of religion. There was the advance of modern industrialism and technology. There was finally the tragedy of the two world wars in the present century, wars which have long left their mark upon the European scene. But amidst all this change the reality of Europe is not destroyed, and the voice of Europe seems to cry: 'Turn back, O Man, forswear thy foolish ways.'

There are those in every country who would see the future to lie not with Christianity but with the creed often described as Scientific Humanism. If I understand them rightly the exponents of this creed hold that by the development of the sciences and by their intelligent application to human affairs the human race will become better organized, more happy, more enlightened, more prosperous, and probably more ethical in its behaviour. It is urged that Religion is to be rejected as it is alleged to hinder the path of progress in two ways. It is said that Religion encourages an unwholesome otherworldliness which causes people to seek another world rather than apply themselves intelligently to the problems of this world. It is also said that Religion encourages anti-scientific attitudes and so hinders the growth of the scientific spirit.

In reply to Scientific Humanism Christianity speaks. The

voice of Christianity cannot today be in exactly the same tones as in the past. Christians have learnt much since the days of the martyrs of Lyons, or of St Bernard, or of St Francis de Sales. In particular, Christians must now admit that there can be bad religion which exposes itself to the criticisms which I have just described. It is possible for bad religion to produce a kind of pietistic selfish otherworldliness; and it is possible for bad religion to resist the scientific spirit: some painful illustrations of this can be found. Yet having acknowledged these things Christianity can go on to make its own radical critique of Scientific Humanism. It will show that the diagnosis of Man's predicament given by Scientific Humanism is misleading, for Man can advance wonderfully in scientific knowledge and yet remain selfish, insensitive, and cruel, and Man's desperate need is to be reconciled with God his Creator and to share in the divine life which is God's gift. Nothing less is needed than the re-creation of Man in the likeness of Christ who is the true Man. The saints of Europe witness that this re-creation of Man is possible; for they were, and are, men and women who were made Christ-like by the power of God.

My plea therefore is that while the Christianity of the future will have a greater sensitivity to the practical needs of humanity and a greater openness to the scientific spirit, it will still be the supernatural faith by which the first Europe was created. It will be the faith that God created Man in his own image with an eternal destiny in heaven as his true goal; that Man has through sin lost the vision of God and entangled himself and the world in frustrations; that Jesus Christ, true God and true Man, was born, lived, died, and rose again and gave the gift of the Holy Spirit in order that Man might be drawn into that fellowship with God which is his true life. In St Augustine's words: 'So deep had human pride sunk us that only divine humility could raise us up.' Today, through the word of Christ and the Holy Spirit and the sacraments, men and women and children may be drawn into one divine life and be set upon the path of humility and charity which leads towards heaven. But because love is one and indivisible, the path towards heaven is also the path of the urgent service of humanity here and now. It is for men and nations to use the earth's resources not as exploiting them for the advantage of individual or nation or race but as developing them for the good of all and for the glory of the Creator. The Christianity of tomorrow must therefore be utterly otherworldly in its belief about Man's destiny and the heavenly perspective of his existence, and at the same time utterly thisworldly in its insistence that to serve suffering humanity is to serve Christ himself.

Christianity has thus its urgent role in the Europe of tomorrow. As it fulfils this role it will be finding new tasks in the contemporary scene. One of its tasks will be to restore the true role of the Family. Family life is at the heart of a healthy society, and no tragedy in the contemporary world is greater than the erosion of family life. Here is a great role for the Christian Church to play. Another of the tasks will be in respect of Race. Racial discrimination is utterly contrary to the teaching of Christianity about the dignity of Man, and on this the witness of the Church must be uncompromising. Another task is in the sphere of affluence and poverty. The Third World knows poverty, hunger, and in too many places starvation. Other parts of the world know comparative affluence. A Christian Europe will not be a Europe which is content to enjoy a high standard of living while others are in poverty; it will be a Europe which serves the world's needs and shares the world's burdens.

In these ways the tasks of Christianity in Europe will touch every human need and human problem. But amidst all these tasks, and giving meaning to them all, there will be the supreme task of bringing men and women and children into the life of fellowship with God along the path of holiness, the path which the saints of Europe painfully and joyfully trod. So there may be born a new Christian humanism. The old Christian humanism blended together the sense of the dignity and beauty of Man belonging to the Graeco-Roman world with the sense of Man's frailty and creatureliness drawn from the Hebraic and biblical faith. It was a tragedy when Christianity and humanism went apart. The new Christian humanism will blend the supernatural faith concerning God and Man with an openness to the sciences, knowing that, amidst all the tensions between imperfect apprehensions of Truth, all Truth is of God and no Truth is to be feared.

From thoughts about Christianity in Europe I turn to thoughts more specifically about the Christian Church.

The older Europe thought of itself, inaccurately and yet plausibly, as coterminous with Christendom. We who are Christians in Europe today are unlikely to forget that Christianity in

Europe is but a small fraction of Christianity throughout the world. On every continent Christianity is to be found. It is misleading to see it as a primarily European phenomenon. The Second Vatican Council reflected vividly the more-than-European character of the Roman Catholic Church. The Lambeth Conference of Anglican bishops in 1968 reflected the more-than-European character of the Anglican Communion. Other Churches have had a like experience. Christian leadership in the world arises from many countries and races. So the European Christianity of the future may not be the 'leading' Christianity in the world. The Holy Catholic Church of the future will involve itself with many national cultures, but it will identify itself with none.

Today there exist within Europe the Roman Catholic Church with its rock-like faith and continuity, the Holy Orthodox Church with its deep grasp of the Communion of Saints, the Protestant Churches of the sixteenth-century Reformation, the Anglican Communion with the See of Canterbury as its symbolic centre; and this does not exhaust the list. Today the impact of the ecumenical movement upon all of them has brought about a new relationship. Old loyalties have not been abandoned, and they continue with their tenacity. But the old 'triumphalist' attitudes have gone, never to reappear. There is the awareness of the unity in Christ of all who share in the one Baptism in the name of the Blessed Trinity. In this awareness there is a working together, a studying together, a praying together, of a new kind.

Within this context I gratefully recall the growing relations between the Roman Catholic Church and the Anglican Communion, symbolized by the Common Declaration signed by Pope Paul VI and the Archbishop of Canterbury in the Basilica of St Paul-without-the-Walls in March 1966. I would refer also to the lecture given by Cardinal Willebrands in the library of Lambeth Palace in October 1972 when he set forward the vision of the Anglican Communion as united with Rome without being absorbed by Rome, a concept which sounded revolutionary when it was put forward in the Malines Conversations by Dom Beauduin with the title 'L'Église Anglaise unie non absorbée'. I recall with no less gratitude the continuing and growing friendship between us Anglicans and the Reformed Churches in France and other countries.

6 Leaving for a lecture tour in Canada, 1971

7 With the Mayor and the City's religious leaders, having received the key to the City of New York, 1974

The message of Pope John XXIII, however, was that unity is inseparable from renewal. The drawing of Churches together can happen only through their being renewed both in inward spirituality and in vigorous service towards mankind. The credibility of the Christian faith in the Europe of the future turns upon there being Christians who show by the Christ-likeness of their lives that Christ is living and true. While spiritual revival is indeed happening within the institutional Church, it is also seen in movements which are impatient with the institutional Church and seek Christian fellowship and social action in experimental groups outside the Church. In many ways, both within and without the institution, the Spirit of God is blowing powerfully today. But true Christianity will hold together the faithful of today with the saints of past ages as the Church witnesses to truth which is timeless and to the things which are not shaken. The saints of Europe now in heaven are near to us, and their prayers help us in our conflict. And among the saints of Europe we may tonight think specially of the martyrs here in Lyons. In the Christian literature of all time there are few passages more moving than the letter from some of the Christians in Vienne and Lyons who survived, written to tell their fellow-Christians in Asia Minor of the manner in which the martyrs had died. 'Regarding their many trials as a small thing they hastened to Christ, truly showing that the sufferings of this present time are not worthy to be compared with the glory that shall be revealed.' There is the Spirit by whom Christianity once conquered, and the Spirit by whom Christianity will conquer still.

The Cost of Pentecost

I will pray the Father, and he will give you another Comforter.
John 14.15

I greet you all, my fellow-Christians, on this great day in the Christian year.[1] We rejoice today in the greatest gift which could ever be given to us. Whitsunday is part of the answer to the child's question: 'Where is God?' It is a question which needs to be asked and answered three times. Where is God? God is above us, about us, around us, the Creator upon whom all existence depends. Where is God? Jesus is God, Jesus is divine, the perfect image of God in history. Where is God? God is within you, the divine Spirit whom Jesus promised. God within you enables you to know, to respond to, to love, and to serve God above and around you. We recall today how the gift promised by Jesus came to the Church on the day of Pentecost in over-whelming power. No eye has ever seen the Holy Spirit or ever can. He is likened by the biblical writers to wind, fire, water: the wind of a mighty gale; the fire which warms to love, to vision, to enthusiasm; the water which drenches hard soil and makes it soft and fruitful. These images describe what the Holy Spirit does in human lives.

Today, however, I would speak to you not about these descriptions of the Holy Spirit but about the *cost* of his coming. If we realize what the cost of the gift was and is to our Lord, we may better understand what it costs us to make the gift our own and to let it have true effect for ourselves.

Jesus is recorded as saying in the discourse at the Last Supper: 'I will pray the Father, and he will give you another Comforter.' The gift, like other gifts of God, is an answer to prayer: in this case the prayer of Jesus. But what sort of prayer was it? The prayer of our Lord which enabled the Holy Spirit to come to the apostles, and to come to us, was not just the speaking of a few words to the Father. No, it was the total offering of himself to the

[1] Sermon preached in Canterbury Cathedral, Whitsunday, 1973.

Father's will and glory, the surrender of the self which is the heart of the prayer of Jesus. So before the account of the supper is ended there come the words of the 'high-priestly prayer', as we call it, when Jesus dedicates himself to his coming death: 'Father, glorify thy Son, that thy Son may glorify thee. . . . For their sakes I consecrate myself, that they also may be consecrated in truth.' Leaving the upper room, Jesus goes on to the garden of Gethsemane and there too he prays: 'Father, if it be possible, let this cup pass from me . . . nevertheless, not what I will but what thou wilt be done.' Then, on Calvary, there is the climax of the self-giving of Jesus, as he moves right into the darkness of the world's tragedy. Such was the prayer of Jesus, the prayer of his self-sacrifice. From this prayer, from this self-sacrifice, there flows the gift of Holy Spirit to the disciples.

Recall two scenes which depict this.

1. When Jesus has died on Calvary the Fourth Gospel tells of how a soldier pierces his side with a lance, and from his side there flows water and blood. The evangelist tells this as an event. But it is also a symbol. Water and blood are cleansing and life, the Spirit's gifts, the Spirit's meaning. So, in symbol, from our Lord's crucifixion the power of Holy Spirit, cleansing and life-giving, flows to us.

2. When Jesus comes to the disciples on Easter evening, as the Fourth Gospel again records, he greets them and shows them the wounds in his hands and his side; and it is immediately after showing them the wounds that he breathes on them and says: 'Receive Holy Spirit.' It is from our Lord's complete sacrifice, from Calvary and Easter, that the Holy Spirit is given. The Cross and the Holy Spirit go together, for the Holy Spirit is the Spirit of Jesus, the Spirit of Calvary and Easter, the Spirit of self-sacrifice, the Spirit of losing life to find it. *That* is the power like wind, and fire, and water. We recall that Jesus said that the Holy Spirit would 'glorify' him; and the Holy Spirit brings to us the glory of Jesus, the self-giving love in which he lived, died, and rose again.

Today we long to see spiritual renewal and revival. We hope for it, we pray for it, we work for it. But remember what it costs, to make such a prayer and to receive such a gift. When we pray the Holy Spirit prays in us, helping us in our weakness and interceding 'with sighs too deep for words' (Rom. 8.26, RSV). And he prays in us the prayer 'Abba, Father', the prayer of Jesus, the prayer of obedience, the prayer of sonship (Gal. 4.6; Rom. 8.16). Our prayer is a little sharing in the prayer of Jesus. We ask ourselves what this costs us, in the giving and the receiving.

A Church, a body of Christians, renewed by the Holy Spirit will be a Church in which there is apparent the sacrifice of the Cross and the joy of Easter. It will be a company of Christians who care: care for God in putting him first of all, care for one another in unselfish fellowship, and care for the world in the urgent service of those in need and suffering. God so loved that he gave, gave himself in Bethlehem, on Calvary, at Easter, at Pentecost, gave himself for us and to us, and enabling us so to love that we too will give. It is thus that we know the power which is like wind and fire and water. It is thus that the power of Whitsunday came. Come, Holy Spirit, come.

3
Serving the World

A Happy Christmas

I greet you all on the birthday of Jesus Christ, a happy Christmas.[1]

Why did it happen? It happened because God loves the world, God loves the human race, and when Jesus was born it was God coming as Man to share the life of our human race, coming right within it. Where did it happen? It happened in a stable at Bethlehem. Now it is often said that Jesus Christ came in poverty and lived in poverty. We should not exaggerate this, for we nowhere read that Jesus was destitute or utterly poor. The point is rather that he came in simplicity, and lived in simplicity—no wealth or worldly power. And when he came in simplicity and lived in simplicity he showed that simplicity is God's way and simplicity is the secret of man's happiness and the key to a right scale of values. Christ wanted human lives to have happiness and fulfilment; he hated suffering and injustice, and we often hear of how he healed the sick and how he once fed a great crowd with bread and fishes. But again and again his message was: simplicity. Nothing did he criticize more than the piling up of possessions, and the preoccupation with money. He taught that people matter more than things. People matter. And if there is simplicity of life without the craving for wealth and luxury people can still love each other, serve each other, enjoy each other, with all the fun and all the laughter in the world. On Christmas Day God comes to us in *divine* simplicity. What a message for our country at this time.

Yesterday I was saying that at this time of strain and anxiety and privation Christmas shakes us into realizing what the birth of Christ is like, in a stable without heat or warmth or energy or power. And it shakes us into remembering that while we have our privations there are in the world those whose sufferings are infinitely worse; those who are homeless and those who are very hungry. Today I see Christmas posing another question to us. In our preoccupation with our standard of living, in our interest

[1] A talk on the BBC, Christmas Day, 1973. The piece which follows (pp. 127–8) was given on the BBC three days later.

in money, money, money, in our expecting to have luxuries which were unknown a generation or two back, have we been missing the secret of simplicity, the simplicity which Christmas shows to be divine as well as human?

If we think again about the homeless and the hungry, the message of simplicity hits us. If we think of how the putting right of our own country is inseparable from the putting right of the world, the message of simplicity hits us again. Above all, if we catch today a new vision of Jesus Christ on his birthday, the message of simplicity meets us with divine force. Come to us today, Lord Jesus; as you were born in a stable, be born into our lives and give us your simplicity, your humility, your courage, your compassion, so that we may serve and help one another and share in the joy of your birthday.

A Happy New Year

The other day when I was working in my study there was suddenly a crash, and it was the big picture above the mantelpiece falling down, dislodging the things on the mantelpiece and tumbling to the ground. The reason was that the cord holding it was worn out and it broke. And no wonder, because it had been there holding up the picture for just on fifty years. The picture is an old favourite of mine: I had it in my room as a student and I have it in my study now, fifty years later. It is Perugino's picture of the Crucifixion of Jesus. And it is for me a great picture, because it wonderfully shows a large part of what Christianity means. Christ is seen suffering, suffering terribly: and yet in it there is triumph because love is there transforming it all. We see the victory of self-giving love, of sacrifice. And nothing is, I believe, more characteristic of Christianity than the power, drawn from Jesus Christ, of bringing into the midst of suffering this outgoing love with its note of victory, serenity, even joy. It is one of the most marvellous things in human life. Just when we are downcast by the problem of evil, the problem of good hits us in the eye and overwhelms us.

Christianity makes a kind of twofold attack on suffering in the world. The Christian will hate the sight of suffering in other people and do his utmost to free them from it. So Christians throw themselves into the care for those who suffer in every way they can: the sick, the homeless, the hungry, and those who face persecution or injustice or abominations like torture. But sometimes when suffering comes to him and cannot be escaped, the Christian is called upon, in the spirit of Christ, to use it, transformed by patience, love, sympathy, power, like Perugino's picture. Someone said that Christ fought suffering in other people as if nothing could be made of it, but when it came to him he used it as if everything could be made of it.

Suffering has been hitting us very hard in recent times. In this country it has come the way of all of us in unfamiliar forms, by the blows which hit our warmth, our light, our comforts, our shopping, our travelling. What do we discover? We discover how very trying it is for all of us, but how much more painful it is for some, and immense new opportunities for unselfishness and comradeship appear. Then we remember, what we sometimes complacently forget, that there have all along been people in our own world whose suffering has been far greater—the homeless, the really hungry, and those treated with injustice. We are stirred to renew our caring about the suffering of our fellows. And we renew that Christian vision, seen in Perugino's picture, of how when suffering comes to ourselves we may face it in the spirit of Christ himself. Here is one of Christianity's great opportunities, the secret indeed of a Happy New Year.

Christianity and Violence

In the previous lectures in this series you have had a remarkable body of knowledge and interpretation presented to you concerning the agonizing problems of violence in the contemporary world. While it is a privilege for me to give the concluding lecture,[1] I think I can add little to the store which has been already presented to you. So I will set myself a limited and modest aim. I will try to see how the various factors are related to the perspective of Jesus Christ and the Christian tradition, and I will try to draw some practical guidelines for our own attitudes and actions. It is likely that those who have followed this series will draw very diverse conclusions from it. But it may be possible for us to agree on a number of principles which it would always be wrong to disregard.

Through the centuries probably only a minority of considering Christians have held that Christ's teaching demands the totally pacifist position. I would hold myself that the injunction to turn the other cheek and to offer no resistance to evil, like many other of Christ's injunctions, concerns motive. Faced with a violent attack the follower of Christ must have total selflessness in motive; so far as his own pride or comfort or security is concerned he must be ready to accept death and have no self-concern. But given that selflessness of motive which Christ demands, he may strike, or risk killing, or even kill if his concern is to protect others, whether family, friends, neighbours, enemies, or the community itself. It has been found possible, however hazardous, to strike in defence of others without hatred, anger, or self-concern; and conversely it is possible to be physically passive while bearing anger and hatred. It is such considerations which cause many conscientious Christians not to endorse total pacifism. So too there is Christ's recognition of the State as the organ of order and justice, a recognition which St Paul and St Peter enhanced and developed. Perhaps a stronger argument for total pacifism

[1] This lecture was delivered in Cambridge, 23 February 1972.

is the centrality of the Cross in Christianity with its corollary of the identity of divine sovereignty and sacrificial love. Is it not by the total acceptance of the principle of the Cross that evil in the world is to be overcome? Even here, however, we note that the principle of self-sacrifice can have a variety of manifestations in different contexts, and that in Christ's teaching the doctrine of the divine judgement upon the world's wrongdoing includes the working out of calamity and pain in the disciplines of humility into God's obedience.

I turn now to the concepts, held in the past in non-pacifist Christianity, concerning the just war and the just rebellion. It is well to notice what the theory of the just war has included. St Thomas Aquinas elaborated the theory as embracing seven conditions.

1. The cause fought for must be just.
2. The purpose of the warring power must remain just while the war goes on.
3. The war must be the last resort when peaceful methods have failed.
4. The methods employed must be just.
5. The results for humanity must be expected to be better than if the war had not been fought.
6. The victory of the righteous cause must be assured.
7. The concluding peace must be just.

On this basis Christian consciences have defended wars fought to defend the weak against aggression or oppression or to overthrow tyranny. Yet where the theory is accepted in the main, the hazards are always immense: the hazard that a war waged with idealistic motives may see those motives corrupted as the process goes on, and the hazard that the outcome may be unpredictable—as if to say, 'It will be a just war if we win it.' We shall see presently what happens to this concept when it moves into the catastrophic conditions of our modern world.

Alongside the tradition of the just war there has been the no less respectable tradition of the just rebellion. In the apostles' teaching the State has a divine function to uphold law, order, and justice; but it is a function exercised under God's supreme authority. And there are two ways in which the State may vitiate its function and stultify its claim to obedience. It may deify itself by claiming an ultimacy which it does not possess. It may so practise injustice as to make its proper role unrecognizable. Hence there emerged an orthodox doctrine of the just rebellion similar in form to the doctrine of the just war. I quote St Thomas Aquinas:

> On the third point it must be said that a tyrannical regime is not just, since it is not directed towards the common good but towards the private good of the ruler . . . and therefore the violent overthrow (*perturbatio*) of such a regime does not partake of the nature of sedition—unless perhaps the violence involved is so extreme that the mass of the governed suffer more harm from the ensuing upheaval than from the rule of the tyrant. A tyrant is rather himself guilty of sedition, inasmuch as he fosters discord and strife among the people subject to him so that he can more safely dominate them.

Do not these words have a very contemporary ring? In subsequent history, however, Roman Catholic teachers have made little appeal to the just rebellion theory, being more concerned to uphold existing orders; and only a very mild suggestion of the just rebellion as a possibility was made by Pope Paul's Encyclical *Populorum Progressio* in March 1967. Meanwhile, however, the concept has come to have a familiar place in democratic social theory. No document is more symbolic of this, or had more influence, than the American Declaration of Independence. I quote:

> Whenever any Form of Government becomes destructive of these ends, it is the Right of the People to alter or abolish it, and to institute new Government, laying its foundation on such principles and organizing its powers in such forms as then shall seem most likely to effect their safety and happiness.

This declaration, which owed its inspiration to Thomas Paine, brings the just rebellion within democracy's lawful pursuits, for how else do you alter or abolish a regime which is destructive of man's proper ends?

It is with these traditions in its thinking that Western Christendom has passed through the centuries and entered the modern world.

Now I ask what is happening in the modern world to these traditional concepts.[1]

First, the older doctrine of the just war has become difficult to uphold with conviction, not impossible in any context perhaps, but difficult. We may still think of possible limited wars to which criteria of justice might be applied; but Vietnam with its continuing destruction without winners is no convincing illustration. When, however, the weapons of war are such that a possible result of a war is the indiscriminate destruction of nations on either side and perhaps the doom of all civilization, how do the old criteria apply? It is partly this consideration which has given a big impetus to total pacifism in recent times. More Christians are convinced pacifists than used to be the case. And the increase of what may be called 'near pacifism' is greater still.

Second, there has been within movements for social change or revolution a rise of the ideology of non-violence. Perhaps this is the reflection within states and countries of the pacifist trend about relations between states and countries. Gandhi in India, Chief Luthuli in South Africa, and Martin Luther King in America have all been instances of this. I think that a range of different ideas has been at work amongst these movements and their leaders, at one end the religious idea that to witness and to suffer patiently is itself a spiritual power by which evil is overcome, and at the other end ideas more akin to a general strike or a mass protest, the ideas that the right course is to upset the community by weight of numbers while avoiding any killing or causing pain. In neither case have we seen the end of these ideas or their application, whether martyrdom in the spirit of the Cross of Christ or protest in the spirit of a general strike.

Third, while in both these ways the non-violent attitudes have grown considerably, there has also been the upsurging of new demands for violent revolution as both a good idea to hold and a good thing to do. Nothing accelerated this more than the story of Mandela and his friends in South Africa. Long, patient use of non-violent methods failed; and they were crushed by the regime's own use of violence. So they asked: 'What then is left

---

[1] I am in this lecture dealing only with forms of violence which might belong to the categories of just war or just rebellion, and not with the violence (so sadly common today) which aims at expressing protest or advertising causes, or giving vent to hatred or cruelty.

to us but violence?' The situation fitted pretty closely to St Thomas Aquinas's classic words which I quoted a few minutes ago: 'the violent overthrow of such a regime does not partake of the nature of sedition'. But inevitably there is the anxiety lest rebellion in desperate circumstances may issue in enhanced suffering for the very people it is designed to help: as St Thomas says in the other words I quoted: 'unless perhaps the mass of the governed suffer more harm from the ensuing upheaval than from the rule of the tyrant'.

So we have seen in relation to the world scene an increasing pacifist trend within Christian thought, overtaken by a revival of the doctrine of violence in relation to particular situations. It is in this scene that we have to make our own decisions as Christians about right and wrong. There are probably many of us who in world terms veer towards pacifism, as there can be no just holocaust; and then feel the case for just rebellions in more limited contexts. What are we to think or do?

I suggest first that we must avoid positions which are so inconsistent as to involve a kind of Pharisaism. We cannot applaud Europeans who resisted the tyranny of a Hitler and then be shocked when Africans want to resist a tyrannical regime today: we can discuss the wisdom or the expediency, but we cannot indulge in facile moral censures. We too easily form a habit of exculpating the violence in our own sphere of history and censuring the violence of other races.

Then, we need to avoid a selective mentality in our moral judgements generally. There are reasons, which I shall mention presently, for our concern about white racism through our own involvement in it. But we need to remember that there are African countries where tribal majorities are unjust to tribal minorities, and where killing and suffering have had appalling dimensions. We need to remember the sufferings, which still continue, of Christians and Jews and others under Communist regimes in eastern Europe. Neither the right eye nor the left eye alone can easily see the whole field of human suffering and moral judgement.

Then, we need to watch the ways in which we can be involved in ethical situations not only by our actions but also by our inactions. Let me give one instance. In the matter of the World Council of Churches grants to combat racism I approved generally the act of identifying with oppressed populations, but I criticized the grants in those two or three instances where the organization assisted was one with a militant purpose, and I maintain my criticism. But if it is wrong to bless a guerrilla movement it is no less wrong tacitly to uphold a regime which uses violence towards its population. This compels us to ask ourselves questions about our practical relations with such regimes.

Then, we cannot honourably commend to other people idealistic Christian actions which we ourselves are unwilling to practise or share. This error can take two forms. We can encourage people to belligerence while ourselves keeping out of the conflict, or we can say to other people that of course their Christian calling is to suffer patiently in the spirit of the Cross of Christ. In either case we can safely say anything at all only if we are ready to be one with those who are suffering. It is this that is imperative; it is also this that is sometimes so hard as to be near-impossible. That is our tragic situation.

So I put to you these guidelines. They do not answer our questions, but at least they can sheer us away from those ethical absurdities which make a right judgement impossible.

Let me illustrate these issues of moral decision from the problem of South Africa. I will not now recall the impressions borne upon me by my own visit to South Africa fifteen months ago when I tried to encourage and befriend those churchmen who are witnessing bravely to humanity and to some of the direct implications of the gospel upon which the South African regime tramples. You had in an earlier lecture in this series the testimony of one whom his fellow-churchmen hold in love and honour, and I cannot doubt that his appraisal will have helped you in your understanding of the tragedy.

First, there is the place of South Africa in our consciousness. I agree with those who say that in a world filled with many varieties of evil and injustice it is wrong for us to become obsessed with any one particular country. Yet South Africa is bound to loom large in our consciousness because its regime claims to be a bastion of Christian civilization and to represent Christian civilization on the African continent, and also because South Africa is the most tragic outcrop of a phenomenon in which we all share, the phenomenon of white supremacy in history. We

8   With Brother Roger Schutz and a group of young people at Taizé, 1973

9 With Mr Vorster in Pretoria, 1970

10 With Dr Anthony Barker at the Charles Johnson Hospital, N'gutu, Zululand, 1970

are part of an era of history in which the white man has been supreme, and can tacitly be sharing in the assumptions of that superiority. Southern Africa is the part of the world where that supremacy is challenged, and is resisting the challenge with violence.

Then we must realize that any attitude on our part towards either violent or non-violent policies is going to be very costly for us if we try to be Christian. If we say to Africans, 'Do not act rashly, a violent revolution is likely only to bring to yourselves terrible suffering', we are saying in effect, 'Go on accepting your present suffering', and we can say that to any people only if we somehow are ready to suffer with them. If we say, 'Why don't you fight?', then we may be advocating something we may not our-selves be aloof from, something which could be a widespread war with hazards about its outcome. In either case our opinions will be Christian and ethical only if we are ready to identify our-selves, and somehow to share in the pains of it all.

Again, we may urge that the best chance for social change lies not through war or the ostracism of any regimes, but through contact with all the influences that may come through social and trade relationships. If so, we must remember that there are forms of contact which help the situation and forms of contact which do not. It does not help when white immigrants go and fill the jobs which should be filled by skilled Africans. It does not help to make investments, unless such investment is designed, as is sometimes possible with difficulty, to help African advancement. It does not even help, as some of the Churches in Southern Africa have found, to subsidize education, unless it is for an educational syllabus which aids advancement and not downgrading. I believe that contact rather than ostracism can achieve something; but it needs to be contact in the right way and with the right care. Otherwise contact may only serve the bolstering up of injustice.

One other issue, paternalism. We need to understand both the big role it has played, not ignobly, in the past, and its obsoleteness today. In the earlier years of the development of Africa as the un-known continent the paternalistic spirit of Christian missionaries did a great work, with qualities of love, care for persons, self-sacrifice, and heroism. That is why there are good Christians today in Africa and elsewhere who find it hard to shed the paternalistic assumptions of their own past. We need to understand this. But while paternalism is understandable as a hang-over, it has no future now. As Bishop Muzorewa from Rhodesia said the other day: 'They say I am a revolutionary; I thought I was a person.' 'I thought I was a person': that is the voice of the future.

The holding of this course in Cambridge itself is a sign of hope for the future. For the hope lies in the existence of Christian men and women who know that these questions about violence and non-violence are crucial for humanity, who do not claim to know all the answers but are passionately keen to try to find answers which are both intellectually serious and congruous with the Spirit of Christ. I have done no more than suggest to you some of the pitfalls of inconsistency to be avoided and some of the paths to be followed. I believe that if we follow these paths we may often discover in particular situations what the Spirit of Christ who is the Spirit of truth will show us if we ask in integrity of mind and sincerity of prayer. Some differences of view may never be resolved, or not resolved for a long time. If my own view is, as it is, not the view of total pacifism, I shrink from commending it to you as the one Christian view, as I remember that two of the best Christians I ever knew personally differed about this. William Temple was, very gently, a non-pacifist. Charles Raven was, violently, a pacifist. In either case we are called upon to be without concern for our own selves, to be ready to identify ourselves with those who suffer, to be undiscriminating in our distributing of moral censures, and to be sure that our strivings for justice and humanity will have fulfilment in a world beyond this. To emphasize the otherworldly goal of Christianity is no escapism, no slackening of our hope for God's reign here in this world. Rather does it give us the true perspective of our present conflicts, showing us that many of our judgements can only be relative, that we never know as much as we think we know, and that every man, woman, and child created by God is eternally in God's keeping, as we look to a day when we shall love as we are loved and know as we are known.

Gandhi

The light shines in the darkness, and the darkness has not overcome it.   *John 1.5, RSV*

We who are Christians proclaim that Christ is the perfect and
final revelation of God, 'God of God, light of light', as we say
in our Creed. At the same time we reverence the divine image in
every man, and we believe that the divine light has shone in
good men of other religions and wherever that light shines we
know we are on sacred ground. It was in that spirit that I as a
Christian went barefoot to the tomb of Gandhi when I was in
India seven years ago. Tonight, while this service in St Paul's
is an act of Christian worship, we join with those of many creeds
who recall the memory of Gandhi with love and honour.

In this service[1] we sang two hymns which Gandhi specially
loved, 'Lead kindly Light' and 'When I survey the wondrous
Cross'. 'Lead kindly Light': the words are so familiar, but how a
man like Gandhi brings out the meaning—when a man sees truth
he follows it fearlessly wherever it leads; when a man has a
conscience he does his best to have it enlightened and then
follows it fearlessly wherever it leads. That was Gandhi. 'When I
survey the wondrous Cross': we Christians survey the Cross of
the Son of God and it is at the heart of our faith. But how hard
it is to put into practice the sacrifice of self in utter self-forgetful
simplicity. We learn from those who have really done that, and
that was Gandhi.

How providential it was to have such a man at such a time.
The vast population of India with its religious fervour, its coming
into control of its own destiny, its deep divisions, its terrible
poverty, in its midst had a leader who every day of his life made
non-violence his ideal, put simplicity of life before wealth and
comfort, put the things of the spirit before material things, made
the cause of the poor and outcast his own, and sealed it all by
a martyr's death. What a gift he was to India!

[1] A commemoration of Gandhi in St Paul's Cathedral, 30 January 1969.

It was not to India alone that Gandhi was a gift, and is today a lesson and a challenge. We talk about spiritual values, but material things easily fill our minds and our activities. How Gandhi shows us the happiness of the way of simplicity. We have a world where violence seems to increase, and the meeting of violence by violence seems the order of the day. How Gandhi shows what non-violence can achieve. We have a world where the voice of conscience, the voice of moral authority is mixed with so many voices of compromise and expediency, and doing right for the sake of doing right is often far to seek. How Gandhi shows us the rule of conscience in the affairs of men. On the mount in Galilee Christ said: 'Blessed are the poor in spirit'; 'Blessed are peacemakers'; 'Blessed are those who hunger and thirst after righteousness'. It was that part of Christ's teaching which appealed to Gandhi. It was that part of Christ's teaching which he followed.

The light shone, and the darkness did not overcome it. We greet today the peoples of India, praying that they may have the peace, the unity, the justice for which Gandhi worked and died. And we pray for ourselves that to us this same light will shine and we shall follow it.

The Death Penalty

The Murder (Abolition of Death Penalty) Bill which was passed in 1965 abolished the death penalty, with the provision that abolition would last only for five years unless meanwhile a resolution was carried by both Houses of Parliament to make the abolition permanent. The speech here reproduced in substance was made in the House of Lords on 20 July 1965, when the Bill passed its second reading by 204 votes to 104. The Resolution whereby abolition became permanent was passed on 18 December 1969.

I believe that retribution is a necessary and valid aspect of punishment. I should wish to emphasize that retribution need not imply vindictiveness or hatred or vengeance. It does mean that the wrongdoer suffers punishment because he deserves to; and the recognition on his part that he is getting something he deserves is a necessary step towards his reformation. And if the crime has been a terrible one, the penalty will be a terrible one.

But in trying to set out what I believe to be Christian principles in this matter, I go at once to two other considerations. First, there ought to be beyond the penalty the possibility of reclamation. I mean the possibility of the person being alive, repentant, and different. If this can happen in this world, and not only for the world to come, we should strive for that to be so. Secondly, there ought to be recognition of the fact that the taking of life as a penalty does devalue human life. It means society saying, in effect: 'This man has killed someone. Very well; we will kill him too.' This does not enhance the sacredness of human life. I believe that it devalues it further.

I am very conscious that these considerations have to be weighed against the other consideration which has been so prominent in the discussion yesterday and today—namely, the need for deterrence. Terrible crime needs to be deterred. Victims must be protected, and all of us feel to the uttermost for victims and their families. If there were convincing evidence that any penalty is a unique deterrent, then I should feel obliged to let that weigh very heavily in the scale against those basic considerations which I have tried to set out. I will come back to that issue later.

Now it is asked: if not the death penalty, then what? I take up my own phrase, 'a terrible punishment for a terrible crime'. Here the arguments seem to me to be very strong for the life sentence rather than a judicial sentence for a certain term of years. There is the argument that the judge cannot know at the outset what the man is going to be like after nine, ten, eleven, or twelve years, or how he should be best treated, both for public safety and for his own good, after that time. That consideration is a strong one, and it concerns both security and the protection of the people, as well as what is good in the reclamation of the criminal himself.

But I would add this consideration, too, in connection with the life sentence. The sentence for the crime of murder ought, I believe, to have what I call a retributive moral seriousness about it: therefore, I believe that the life sentence is right, even though it again and again, and perhaps almost always, be mitigated in practice. The life sentence says, in effect, to a convicted murderer: 'You have outraged society by killing one of your fellows. You must expect no claim to your old place in society for a very long time, not, indeed, until society can be told that you are on the way to being a different sort of person from what you are now.' I believe that, thus understood, a life sentence carries with it a moral meaning.

Yesterday the Lord Chief Justice pleaded for far fuller consideration of the life sentence and the procedures in connection with it. Indeed, it should in some cases be a really long sentence for desperate types of criminal. But he urged, also, that the penal methods ought to be such—and I am glad he said that he was sure they could be such—that personality should not rot in the process. But I wonder whether, in trying by amendments to this Bill to give further definition to the content of a life sentence, we are any more likely to be successful than they were in another place. The life sentence is a deterrent because it can demand the custody of the person for a very long time, and it carries with it the right of the State to recall the person to custody. It should be reformative. There is ample evidence that already it can prove reformative; indeed, we can most certainly hope for means in the future to make it so. For all these reasons, I believe that the alternative to capital punishment should be defined as the life sentence rather than the various alternatives which have been tried and pleaded for.

Let me come now to the special problem of the Homicide Act. Previous to the Homicide Act there had been attempts to get at a classification of murders, with some moral distinction between those which were more loathsome or more morally vicious than others. In a debate here in 1947 my predecessor, searching as others at the time were searching for some line of distinction between capital and non-capital murders, spoke of the distinction between 'murder' and 'murder most foul'. But when the Homicide Act drew a distinction, it did not claim to be a moral distinction in that way. It drew a distinction, on lines of expedience and of public safety, between murder in circumstances where the death penalty might be a unique deterrent to violence or the use of arms, and murder in circumstances where that was not so. It was Lord Conesford who said in his speech on the second reading of the Homicide Bill that a moral issue was involved, and that the proposed distinction between capital and non-capital murders would be found to affront morality—though he then made it clear that he was not an abolitionist. I said at that time, in a brief intervention, that I agreed with him.

Now, two successive Home Secretaries, different in their politics and different in their initial approach to the abolition question, have told how they have found intolerable moral issues in the distinction of sentence between capital and non-capital murder. On the one hand, a murderer kills while stealing, perhaps on a sudden, delirious impulse—the death penalty. On the other hand, a murderer poisons after loathsome, vicious premeditation—not the death sentence. If penalties other than the death penalty were involved, the moral arbitrariness of the distinction might be swallowed. But where the penalty is sometimes to kill the murderer, and sometimes not, it seems that law and morality have gone apart on the very point where it is imperative for them to go together. It was not surprising to hear from the Lord Chief Justice yesterday: 'I have seen the complete absurdities that are produced, and have been completely disgusted at the result.' To be fair, these considerations may be construed as an argument for going back, as well as an argument for going forward to total abolition. But I was impressed to hear yesterday from the Lord

Chief Justice the plea that to go back to the older system of general capital sentences, mitigated by frequent reprieves, was to put a quite intolerable burden upon the mind and heart of the one man on whom it falls to make those decisions.

I realize, and I feel deeply, that against all these considerations the argument of a unique deterrence in the death penalty might throw an overwhelming weight if it were an argument that had real validity. Like others, I have been very worried about this and ready to let the evidence have all the weight that it might have. I have not the training of a lawyer, but I can read and listen, like any person who might be eligible to sit upon a jury in this country. After listening and reading a great mass of evidence, I feel that there is a dearth of convincing evidence that for murders by armed thieves the death penalty is a unique deterrent. There has been such opportunity for the production of that evidence, in weighty and convincing forms, in these last two days, and I do not feel it has been there. In its place, we have had generalizations and appeals to feelings—feelings, of course, which we all have, and which cannot help moving us.

There is the evidence, on the other side, of the former Home Secretary, Mr Henry Brooke: 'By no means all those murderers who came before me because they had been sentenced to death were from the criminal classes.' There is the evidence as to the proportionate increase in murders now capital and murders not capital since the Homicide Act became law. The figures here show that the increase has been in both categories, thereby combating the view that the death penalty is a uniquely powerful deterrent. We do not think to look to the evidence of foreign countries in order to be impressed by this evidence which we have at home, although I believe that some of the evidence from foreign countries is, when sifted, very weighty indeed. I could not help being impressed by the speeches yesterday of no fewer than three of Her Majesty's Judges who were, in a way, giving their own evidence and also summarizing their weighing of the general evidence of people and situations, which is their life's work. I could not help being impressed by their conclusions, and it is not shown that the death penalty is a uniquely powerful deterrent.

Let me end by referring to those considerations of feeling which bear upon us, whatever our conclusions and opinions may be. No one can help feeling terribly for the victims of crime and their families. No one can help feeling terrribly the fears which exist in many hearts since crime, and not least violent crime, has increased. Still more must our feelings go out to the members of the Police Force and to those who are in the Prison Service. The country owes so much—and there is no limit to what it owes—to its servants who are exposed to great dangers in serving it. But again and again in the formation of judgements upon human affairs we have, on the one hand, a set of anxieties, and, on the other, the action or conclusion needed to answer those anxieties. So often we tend to build a bridge from the one set of facts to the other set of facts by our feelings and our emotions, rather than by our reason. Not many years ago, at a time when the increase of violent crime was giving so much anxiety, we were urged to build the bridge between the anxieties and the conclusions by the reintroduction of flogging. It was really a method of substituting feeling and emotion for reasoned conviction about causes and effects.

I believe that the issue in this case is somewhat the same, and that here too it is not those emotional considerations but the conclusions of reason which should prevail. I believe it to be a completely reasonable conclusion that capital punishment is not a unique deterrent; that a sentence of life imprisonment is a terrible sentence, deterrent in effect, and capable of issuing in a wise, stern, and human penology, and that to abolish the death penalty in this country will set us in the way of progress in this matter, and rid us from the wrong of a system which punishes killing by a penalty which helps to devalue human life. I therefore hope that the House will give a second reading to this Bill, and that it will soon become the law of this country.

Apartheid

I, if I be lifted up from the earth, will draw all men unto myself.

John 12.32

Tonight I bring greetings from the Cathedral of Canterbury to the Cathedral of Johannesburg.[1] The bonds which unite our Churches within the Anglican Communion are very strong as we pray for one another and try to serve one another. I am now near the end of my visit to the Church of this Province, and my heart has been warmed by the many signs of friendship between us within our wide Anglican family.

My text recalls the stirring scene on Palm Sunday. Our Lord has ridden into the city of Jerusalem on an ass's colt, and there is great excitement in the city. Hitherto his mission has been almost entirely to the people of Palestine of his own Jewish race. But now some people from a far country, Greeks, approach and ask to see Jesus. They put their request to Philip, and he consults Andrew, and when the request reaches Jesus his response is startling. He at once speaks about the death which he is going to die, using the parable of the grain of wheat which has to fall into the earth and die before it can be fruitful. And he adds: 'I, if I be lifted up from the earth, will draw all men unto myself.' The power which will draw the nations to him will be the self-sacrifice of his death, bringing to them both the divine judgement and the divine appeal of love.

The fulfilment of our Lord's prophecy began as soon as the apostles started to preach the message of the Cross, and it has continued through the centuries. Today, while Christians are but a minority in the world and powerful non-Christian or anti-Christian forces exist in many parts of the world, Christians are to be found in every country in the world, and their influence is often far beyond their numbers. Here in this beautiful country there are people of black races and coloured people and Afrikaners

[1] This address was given in St Mary's Cathedral, Johannesburg, on 29 November 1973, at the end of a tour in South Africa.

and English-speaking people who have been drawn to Christ lifted up on the Cross. Each of us who is here tonight will thank God for the wonderful Christian privilege which all unworthily we have received owing to the spread of the gospel far and near.

When, however, our Lord draws people to himself he draws them not as separate individuals or groups but as one Christian fellowship. The Acts of the Apostles and the letters of St Paul describe vividly the character of the Church as the family of Christ. We notice three things:

1. The Christians shared together in the sacrament of the Body and Blood of Christ on every Lord's day. It was the focus of their union with Christ and with one another: 'We being many are one bread, one body, for we all partake of the one bread.'

2. They had in the first age of Christianity no cathedrals or consecrated churches to worship in. It was in one another's houses that they would meet for worship, unless it was sometimes in the open air.

3. The fellowship in one another's houses, both socially and for worship, cut across the barriers of race. We remember how on one occasion at Antioch St Paul severely rebuked St Peter for slipping back from the principle of the races joining in table fellowship. We remember also St Paul's great sentence: 'Welcome one another, as Christ has welcomed you, to the glory of God.' The realization that Christ has welcomed all of us as utterly unworthy sinners will lead us to welcome one another, whatever the race or the colour may be, as fellow-Christians and brother men. St Paul would allow no barrier to cut across that welcome.

Such was the Church in the early days, with the Cross at its centre and with this new, deep, and creative principle of fellowship as its principle. So it began to draw the people to Christ. Here in this Cathedral of St Mary tonight the presence together of men and women and children of different races is a picture of what the Church is meant to be; and Philip and Andrew would rejoice to see the fulfilment of Christ's prophecy which they heard in Jerusalem on Palm Sunday.

So the work of Christ continues. But there are terrible hindrances.

I know about the hindrances in England; and you will know about the hindrances in this country, for every country has them. I think of three ways in which the work of Christ can be most sorely hindered—in each case by division and separation.

1. There are the divisions of Christian denominations. In England this hinders. In every country this hinders. But, thank God, the movement for Christian unity grows. While the problem of union is not yet solved, Christians of different Churches are working together as brother Christians in new ways.

2. There are the strains within the family. The sacredness of the family is at the heart of sound community life, and wherever the family is strained or eroded or disrupted the damage to Christian witness is incalculable. This happens in a number of ways in all our countries through the undermining of Christian morality. One of the ways in which the undermining of the family and of true morality can happen is by an industrial system which forcibly separates wage-earning men from their families for nearly all the year. Such a system, wherever it exists, is utterly at variance with the sacredness of the family and the true character of human community. Ought the Christian conscience to tolerate this?

3. So too the separation of races in churches and in homes and in social life mars the character of Christian fellowship as the apostles understood it. Separation, whether in churches or in the homes of the people, contradicts the doctrine 'Welcome one another as Christ welcomed you'. In every country there is much to repent about. If we exclude a man because he is of another race or colour are we not excluding Christ himself?

Those are some of the ways in which Christ's followers may hinder the fulfilment of Christ's words 'I will draw all men unto myself': divisions of Churches, divisions in families, separation of races in society. But Christ's work continues, and he calls upon us his followers to set it forward and not to hinder it.

Today the world contains terrible problems of human injustice. There are those who look to violence for solving the problems of human injustice, but Christ did not call his followers to violence, and we may shrink from the terrible results which can follow the attempt to solve problems by violence. But the alternative to violence is the making of considerable changes by those who have the power to make those changes, while there is still time. That is the issue.

Those who witness to Christ faithfully are often called to suffer with him, and he promises us that if we do suffer with him we may already share in his joy, 'as sorrowful yet always rejoicing', near to him who was lifted up on the Cross and raised from the dead on Easter morning. Let my final words to those who are in brave conflict with injustice be: Do not be afraid, let the love of Christ drive away fear; and we are told that 'if we suffer with him we shall also reign with him'.

Kenya Asians

In February 1968 the Labour Government introduced the Commonwealth Immigrants Bill for the purpose of restricting the entrance into this country of Kenya Asians who possessed United Kingdom passports. It was held by many, including the former Secretary of State for the Colonies, Iain Macleod, that the Bill implied a breach of faith with people to whom this country had granted citizenship. The substance of a speech in the House of Lords on 29 February 1968 is here reproduced. The House gave the Bill a second reading by 109 votes to 85, and it became law on the following day.

I want to dwell first on the subject of race relations within this country and the effect of this Bill upon those relations. My knowledge of the problems is linked with the fact that for the last two and a half years I have worked with the National Committee for Commonwealth Immigrants. That body has the task of promoting good community relations—I prefer the phrase 'community relations' to the term 'integration'—in the areas where there are immigrants from other Commonwealth countries. The Committee is the centre of a considerable work done throughout the country, in which municipal authorities and many voluntary helpers share. There are thirty full-time officers in different towns and cities, and the London staff of the Committee comprises about thirty people drawn from different races from this country and from other countries. The Government give to the National Committee an annual grant of £170,000; and finance is partly provided by municipalities and partly comes from bodies such as the Gulbenkian Trust.

My own share in the work is not a large one. As Chairman, my role has been no more than to help many different people to work together. But I have been able to learn something about the splendid work that is being done for the building up of good community relations in the towns and cities where tensions exist and where tensions are threatened. In particular, through this organization much has been done in the realm of helping schools to grapple with the problems created by the influx of children from other countries. Much also has been done by voluntary actions in the field of housing—actions to prevent the development of what might be ghettos in some of the cities. Much has also been done to give a friendly help to immigrants to find their way to places where they will be useful and where relations are likely to be happy. And all the time a good deal has been done through these bodies in the education of public opinion on both sides. This means helping immigrants from other countries to understand the ways and customs in the United Kingdom which are unfamiliar to them, and also helping our own English-born citizens to understand the ways, the cultures, and the backgrounds of those who come from other parts of the world.

Inevitably, matters concerning entry into this country react sharply upon the question of integration and good relations in this country. It is often said, and quite rightly, that if the numbers are fewer it is easier to tackle the practical problems. But while that is so largely true, it is also a rather dangerous half-truth in this sense: that if there is a genuine injustice in connection with any matter of entry, then the reaction upon trust and mutual good relations in this country can be very considerable.

Now I come to this Bill. No doubt the Home Secretary thought that if this action was taken to stave off a particular threat of influx the result would be that the problem of race relations and the problem of good community relations in this country would be prevented from being more difficult for those who are grappling with it. But I believe that if he had consulted those whom I have mentioned, who are doing the practical work in many localities, under the aegis of the Government's own appointed National Committee, he would have had rather different advice—advice from which I think he might have benefited in the formulation of policy, and certainly in the psychological mode for the presentation of the policy. I thought that the non-consultation with the National Committee—I do not mean with myself, but with the very skilled persons who are its workers at many levels—very odd.

The fact is that the Bill, and the sudden launching of it on the country, has brought a good deal of dismay to many of those who are working for good community relations, and a good deal of distrust not only among the immigrant communities, where a new handle is being given to the somewhat more extremist elements, but also among those who are trying so hard to get on with this devoted work. Why distrust? Because the Bill virtually distinguishes United Kingdom citizens on the score of race, and because the Bill virtually involves this country in breaking its word.

First, let us take the question of race. Clause 1, on any showing, creates two levels of United Kingdom citizens. Strictly, the level is not that of race; strictly, the grandfather clause means not race, but geography. But the actual effect on the bulk of the human situation with which the Bill is dealing is that the one level is the level of the European and the other level is the level of the Asian citizens. And that is so because the object of the exercise, and the apology for the exercise, is that we must keep an influx of Asian citizens out of the country.

Then the question of the word of this country. The technical arguments have been put the other way: that in strict law the Asians still retain citizenship: they cannot have the citizenship that operates in India, they have not a citizenship that guarantees their coming to this country, but they are still citizens. That is making the word 'citizenship' really a technicality devoid of living content. Much has been made of the argument that the position about citizenship under this Bill is parallel to the position about citizenship under the 1962 Bill, and that those who accept the provisions of the 1962 Bill ought not to complain of the treatment of citizenship under this Bill. I believe that that is logic, but I do not believe it is human reality at all, for the reason that there is all the difference in the world between Commonwealth citizens who, if they do not have a citizenship they can operate here, have a citizenship that can operate somewhere; and, on the other side, persons in Kenya who have not got a citizenship which operates there and were encouraged to have a United Kingdom citizenship in the belief that it would be for them an operative citizenship. And this Bill evacuates it, I believe, from really being an operative citizenship.

For that reason, I do not believe it is a misreading of the situation when we say that the Bill virtually implies a race distinction in citizenship in Clause 1; and that it virtually means the breaking of this country's word. In saying that last thing, I am not meaning that particular statesmen made promises and broke them. No.

What we are saying is that the country, by its total action, involved itself in a certain obligation, and that this Bill abrogates that obligation. For that reason, however much the Bill may be improved between now and the small hours of the morning, there is at the heart of it something that is really wrong.

None the less, there it is. And if we set about the task of improving it, what can be done? First of all, I think we should ask for the removal of the figure of 1,500, not only as a flexible figure but as a figure at all, because it is quite inadequate to the justice of the situation towards a community of Asians who have relied upon us as they have. As to the method of entry, might there not be an office of this country in Kenya which, not simply taking first those who have enough money to come first, would look into the whole matter of why people want to come, what are they going to do when they come, and so on, with a far more scientific and humane handling of the matter? Surely that could have been done if there had not been the disastrous rush.

Secondly, the grandfather element in Clause 1 must, I think, go, because it brings to the Bill that stigma which I mentioned. And thirdly, we want a promise for the full implementation of the Wilson Committee's proposals, not only concerning appeals but also concerning the comprehensive welfare system which was thought at the time to go hand in hand with the system of appeals. It is a good many months since the Wilson Committee made their Report.

I agree wholeheartedly that there is a great deal that can be done in this country, and in connection with other Commonwealth countries, in grappling with this problem. Indeed, in discussion with other Commonwealth countries it might be seen how the skills of Asians at present in Kenya might be used, some in this country, some in other countries—not as a kind of problem, but as human beings with something scientific to contribute to the lives of particular communities, if those communities would shed their particular racial prejudices, whatever they are, and enjoy their help.

But whatever we may do to retrieve the situation, the harm has been done by this Bill. Reference has been made to those who oppose this Bill on abstract grounds. I do not know what the word 'abstract' means: I would say ethical grounds; and ethical grounds are never merely abstract, because ethical grounds

Lc

always have practical consequences, and it is some of the practical consequences in race relations that are dangerous, on account of what is written into this Bill.

That there is an implicit breaking of something seems to be borne out by the great unease about this Bill. I heard that in another place the second reading passed in a kind of sepulchral silence; and I think it will pass, if it does pass, in this House in a very sepulchral silence. Why this unease? It really is an unease, and I believe that it is an unease we all share. We all find this vast human problem too much for us, and there can be no sort of 'more righteous than thou' attitude in any single one of us on this matter.

I think the unease is this. From time to time, on occasions when a great event or a great man is being commemorated, we go across the road to Westminster Abbey. I think the last time that happened was when many of us went to Westminster Abbey for the funeral of Clement Attlee. During that very moving service a psalm was sung, and I think we were all very moved by the way in which the psalm touched us, whatever our religion. The psalm touched us by its accurate, photographic reference to the character of Clement Attlee. In that psalm, with its description of that man, there was the sentence: 'He that sweareth unto his neighbour and disappointeth him not: though it were to his own hindrance'. And that is what lies at the bottom of the unease about this Bill.

Frank Weston of Zanzibar

Jesus Christ is the same, yesterday, today, and for ever.
Hebrews 13.8

It is fitting that St Matthew's should be the place where we commemorate tonight the birth of one who first set out for Africa from a curacy in this parish, and said his goodbye here before he left for Africa for the last time.[1] To the older of us who are here Frank Weston was an inspiration, always vivid, always challenging, always loved, and often uncomfortable. To some of the younger churchmen today he may be a name only. To history, he is a prophetic figure, remarkable in any Christian era. To our Divine Lord, we cannot doubt he is a faithful servant who now reflects his Master's glory, having shown not a few glimpses of that glory in his years on earth.

'Weston, if Jesus asked you for your coat, would you give him your shabbiest coat?' That remark made by one of his early teachers shows the form in which the call of Christ always presented itself to him. If he gave at all, he must give all. So, without abandoning the scholarly interests of a very able pupil of Dr Sanday at Oxford, he found himself first at the Trinity College Mission at Stratford and then as curate here at St Matthew's. In 1898 at the age of 27 he joined UMCA in the diocese of Zanzibar, where he spent the rest of his years, becoming Bishop in 1908. He quickly formed the conviction that in a Church in an African country the people who matter most are the Africans. It is easy to say that, but not every missionary practised it with the thoroughgoing ruthlessness of Frank Weston. He lived as the Africans lived, as one of them. And early in his African time he declared that Africans must everywhere become the leaders of Christianity in Africa. Africans knew him as a very loving and very stern Father-in-God. He was severe in the Church's moral discipline, but always lovingly. The story is told of a public

---

[1] Address given in St Matthew's, Westminster, at the centenary of Frank Weston's birth, 13 September 1971.

excommunication, solemnly pronounced in church: the awful ceremony proceeded, the candles were extinguished, and when the words came, 'We do hereby cut you off,' the Bishop burst into tears as he spoke them. During the war when the British invaded the German territory in East Africa, the Bishop raised and led a carrier-corps for the troops as a major, leading them with great efficiency. It was part of his mission. 'He marched with us, he slept with us, and when we lay down at night, did he not pray with us? And when we rose in the morning, did he not pray with us again? Truly he was a great man.' Injustice to Africans made his blood boil. He attacked the injustices of German rule in a pamphlet, *The Black Slaves of Prussia*. He later attacked injustices on the part of this country in another pamphlet, *Serfs of Great Britain*.

Absorbed in Africa as Frank Weston was he did not let the rest of the world forget him, and specially in the last ten or twelve years of his life the rest of the Anglican Communion took note of him as a fiery controversialist.

First, he fought Modernist tendencies in theology, sending broadsides home, somewhat to the discomfort of Archbishop Randall Davidson, and even to the breaking of communion between his diocese and the diocese of Hereford. Weston had proved himself a deep and constructive thinker in his book *The One Christ*, a treatment of Kenotic Christology adventurous and yet essentially orthodox. His concern about Modernism was that Moslem propagandists against the Christian Faith in East Africa were quoting phrases from Modernist books to denigrate the people's belief in the divine Jesus. This roused Weston to passion.

Second, he fought what he held to be Pan-Protestant tendencies about Christian unity, denouncing those Anglican bishops who had at a conference at Kikuyu in 1914 given Holy Communion to the non-episcopalian participants. The controversy which followed in many parts of the Anglican Communion did not prevent Weston from a sharing in the production of the Appeal for Christian Unity at the Lambeth Conference of 1920, where he showed that a zeal for unity can have more forms than one. It was there that he won the friendship of a man as unlike him in temperament and opinions as possible—Herbert Hensley Henson, Bishop of Durham. Henson wrote of him:

He was, in my belief, a very good unselfish Christian, with all a fanatic's sincerity and all a fanatic's injustice, but by nature entirely lovable. It was impossible not to feel his charm, even when one execrated his bigotry. Something should be added about his practical sagacity, which I think was quite conspicuously great whenever his fanaticism did not cloud his judgement; and something more should be said about his passionate love for souls which carried him into the company of the greater saints.

On the English scene his influence reached its climax at the Anglo-Catholic Congress of 1923, at which he presided. At the closing session in the Albert Hall he held the vast concourse spellbound as, with the title 'Our Present Duty', he spoke of the Christ of Bethlehem whose leaping across the gulf between Creator and creature, holiness and sin, must inspire us in our leaping over barriers and distances in human relationships. He spoke also of the naked Christ of Calvary, appealing for self-sacrifice, discipline, and penitence. He spoke also of the Christ of the Blessed Sacrament, here using controversial words which became notorious:

I beg you, brethren, not to yield one inch to those who would for any reason or specious excuse deprive you of your taber-nacles . . . I want you to make your stand for the tabernacle, not for your own sakes but for the sake of truth first and in the second place for the sake of reunion hereafter.

But his last word was about the Jesus of suffering humanity.

You cannot claim to worship Jesus in the tabernacle unless you pity Jesus in the slum. Go out into the highways and hedges, where not even the Bishops will try to hinder you; go out and look for Jesus in the ragged and the naked, the oppressed and the sweated . . . look for Jesus, and when you see Him gird yourselves with His towel and wash His feet.

Those were the words by which Christians in England came chiefly to remember Frank Weston. But all that was known of him in England was but a tiny fraction of a life and a mission in Africa and for Africa. He said his last goodbye here in St Matthew's in the autumn of 1923. A year later he died in the course of one of his Confirmation tours. Looking back at his life one is conscious of the immense differences which half a century has brought. East Africa, how different with Tanzania, Zambia, Kenya, all independent. The Anglican Communion, how different, first with a single province embracing both Zanzibar and Kikuyu in a kiss of peace, and now with several East African provinces with African leadership. The liturgical scene, how different— and today the language about tabernacles might raise the largest eyebrows not in Lambeth Palace but in many Roman Catholic circles, where the pattern of sacramental life has changed. Different, yes in some ways. But Jesus Christ is the same, yesterday, today, and for ever; and for all time his people need the witness of sacrifice, of selflessness, of penitence, and of joy which shone in Frank Weston of Zanzibar. But it would displease him if we tried to be solemn about him. So let the last word be that of the little African boy who said, 'You know he is a loving man, for his mouth is always opened ready for laughter, for he is still laughing and he will laugh for ever.'

Europe and the Third World

But he, desiring to justify himself, said to Jesus, And who is my neighbour?   *Luke 10.29*

Nearly a year ago this country entered the European Economic Community.[1] Our links of trade with Europe are now far closer, and the hope is held out that we and the other countries of the European community will be more prosperous together than we could be in isolation. But will it be a Christian Europe, a Europe inspired by the teaching of Jesus Christ and the ideals which flow from Bethlehem and Calvary? Will it? The issue is clear. A Christian Europe will be a Europe set upon using its resources in the service of humanity as a whole. Love for neighbour is Christ's law for states and communities as well as for individuals. And we fool ourselves if we see our neighbour just as the people of our own country, or just as the countries near to us in whose trade and well-being we share. If we do that we are perilously like the lawyer who 'desiring to justify himself said to Jesus, And who is my neighbour?'

It was never likely that the Christian ideal of a Europe serving the world would easily come to dominate European attitudes and policies. It is true that statesmen are ready to talk about the service that Europe can give to the world. But when anxiety about our people's own standard of living and economic burdens looms large, as it does just now, even the talk of our duty to the Third World easily disappears. No, if the Christian ideal for Europe is to prevail there must be the continuous pressure of those who believe in that ideal, moulding opinions, attitudes, policies. It means that certain central Christian doctrines must deeply influence the European attitude. There is the doctrine that power is properly linked with service: 'The rulers of the nations lord it over them and are called benefactors, but it shall not be so with you.' There is the doctrine that on this small planet

[1] This sermon was preached in Southwark Cathedral on Sunday, 25 November 1973.

we are all members one of another. There is the doctrine that to serve the man or the woman who is hungry is to serve Christ himself. It is by remembering these truths, and putting them into practice, that we see the difference between a Europe and a Christian Europe.

Europe '73 Programme is a wonderful effort to recall Europe's leaders and Europe's peoples to the meaning of a Christian Europe, a Europe which knows the true answer to the question 'Who is my neighbour?' And a Europe which answers that question will do the practical things which are the least that need doing. It will give easier access to its markets to goods from the poor countries. It will enable continual imports of agricultural produce from poor countries. Those are the two urgent matters of policy. And our country will not be content with less than 0·7% of the gross national product as its figure for official aid. What will the answer be? Pray that it will not be the answer of the lawyer, 'he desiring to justify himself said to Jesus, And who is my neighbour?' It is after all to Jesus that professedly Christian peoples give their answers. And so do we all.

Now it had not been foreseen that Europe '73 Week was going to coincide with a week when every newspaper, every news bulletin, every speech in this country seems to be filled with our own economic anxiety as a country. Is this, people might say, is this a moment to choose? The answer is that Christianity teaches us that when we have troubles of our own we see aright when we see them as part of the wider, vaster troubles of mankind as a whole, and when we remember that there are parts of the world where sufferings are so great that our own can scarcely be called sufferings at all. We in this country are not starving, we are not very poor, we have a high standard of living, we have many luxuries. So try to picture those who have a few mouthfuls for their families to eat every day; a few mouthfuls. Indeed, our own troubles and conflicts might be nearer solution if we had not been so long obsessed by taking our economic temperature over and over again, and so getting our own values wildly wrong. If we at this moment have our troubles, what a chance there is to see them as a little bit of the world's troubles, what a chance to see, to care about, to feel the desperate plight of others in the world. Again and again I find the apostles in the New Testament writings bidding the Christians of their time to think of the greater conflicts, the greater hardships of their brethren in other lands. We are, we really are, members of one another.

While, however, we are pressing for peoples and governments to adjust their sights to a Christian vision and to the consequential Christian obligations, we find the voice of Christ speaking to our own consciences. Am I ready for a simpler way of life, ready for standards less well-to-do than we have had in the past? Do I myself care enough to be doing all I can in the service of the hungry? Do I care in a way that really costs me? The picture comes before us of Jesus approaching the city of Jerusalem and weeping over it as it did not know the things which belonged to its peace. We may picture Jesus today weeping over many cities, towns, villages, and countries: some with their poverty and hunger, some with their wealth, their power, and their complacency. The tears of Jesus unite our world and show us how bound in a bundle we are. Jesus would have us share in his grief, and if we are his followers we shall not wish it otherwise. But those who share in the grief of Jesus are admitted to a share in his joy: his joy over one sinner who mends his ways, his joy over every cup of cold water given to a child who is in need, his joy over every act of true service to his heavenly Father and to mankind. We shall not ask, 'Who is my neighbour?' My neighbour is Christ and Christ is everywhere.

The Three Crosses

This is the victory that overcomes the world, our faith.[1]

1 John 5.5

Christianity is concerned not with one Cross but with three. When our Lord was approaching the final crisis of his life on earth he foretold that three kinds of suffering lay ahead.

There would be his own suffering with its climax in his death by crucifixion. It was a death as terrible as any can be. But it was a death which his followers were one day to hail not only as shame and reproach but as victory and glory. That was the first Cross, the Cross which became the supreme Christian symbol.

There would also be the suffering which Christ's own followers would experience. You remember how he said to the two sons of Zebedee, James and John, 'Are you able to drink the cup that I drink?' The disciples shrank from dying with Jesus, there and then, on Good Friday. But through the years Christians have been called to suffer with Christ, some by dying as martyrs, some by facing persecution, and all by lives of self-sacrifice. Those who have readily suffered with Christ have found that Christ's peace and joy become theirs too in a wonderful way. As one of the apostolic writers said, 'If we suffer with him we shall also reign with him.' That is the second Cross which Jesus foretold.

Then, the third Cross. This would be the suffering of the world which rejected Jesus Christ, the divine judgement when men and nations bring suffering upon themselves and upon their fellows. When they reject the way of love which Jesus taught and turn their backs upon the ceaseless appeals of God to their consciences, calamities follow. So the last loving appeal of Jesus to the people was mingled with the forebodings of judgement; and on the road to Calvary Jesus turns to the women and says: 'Daughters of Jerusalem, weep not for me, but weep for yourselves and your children.' Where there is in the world selfishness, hatred, violence, cruelty, lust, there comes a Cross of human suffering, dark and

[1] A sermon preached in Canterbury Cathedral, Easter 1970.

bitter, with none of the radiance of Calvary to lighten it. That is the third Cross which Christ predicted.

Easter is now speaking. 'This is the victory that overcomes the world, our faith.' Jesus died, Jesus rose again, Jesus lives. And he has called us who are known as Christians to follow him, to live in fellowship with him, to share in his joy and his victory. That is the message of Easter. But it is not a message which tells us that suffering is ended. No, the Easter message has as its context the stark realities of our suffering world. Amidst these stark realities Jesus summons us to follow him, and he tells us that as we do so we are likely to have trials and pains in plenty, the trials and pains of the second of the Crosses. But it will be different, different because we shall be with Jesus and his joy and peace will be with us. We shall be working with Jesus to rescue the world from the third Cross, the Cross of judgement and alienation, of human selfishness and misery.

So Easter says to us: Have faith. Faith does not mean that we first try to see things in a coherent and intelligible shape and then conclude that God is true. Faith is more like when the women came to the tomb when it was still very dark, and they wondered who could move the stone as it was very heavy: and look, the stone is gone. When things are very dark, when human possibilities are exhausted, when we are at the end of our tether, God acts. Easter defines for all time the character of Christian faith: human weakness, divine power; I can't, God can; I am weak, God is strong; I am a sinner, God forgives. Does this sound fanciful? It was such a faith which made the apostles carry the gospel into a hostile world. It was such a faith which sustained Christian men and women again and again through the centuries. It is like a coin which is always on one side frailty, penitence, death, and on the other side power, forgiveness, life. Let the words of St John sound in our hearts today: 'This is the victory that overcomes the world, our faith.'

The Christian Church needs to live by faith and by faith alone. This means that it will not look for success or power as the world assesses success or power, but that it forgets success or power as it cares supremely about the God in whom it trusts and about the people whom it serves with compassion in God's name. Possessing such a faith the Church will have its imagination stirred in its witness against evil and injustice, in its indifference to irrelevant values, and in its faithfulness to the Cross. Inspired by the first Cross, the Church will accept for itself the way of the second and help in the world's deliverance from the miseries which come from selfishness and fear.

There is still today the Cross of the world's sin and misery when it turns its back upon God's righteousness. Let us proclaim that a country which rejects God's laws brings judgement upon itself. Where there is the selfish pursuit of pleasure with insensitivity to the needs of others, where there is the erosion of family life as the heart of a sound society, where there is racial discrimination, where there is violence and cruelty, there the judgement of God falls and Jesus weeps over the city that does not know the things that belong to its peace.

There is still the Cross of those who try to follow our Lord faithfully. It makes all the difference if our griefs and pains and disappointments are shared with our Lord, and if we realize the privilege of sharing a little in *his* grief as he shares and bears the world's grief. The words are vividly true: 'In the world you have tribulation, in me peace.'

Above all, we fix our eyes on the Cross where Jesus died, died in desolation, died in glory. And near where they crucified him was a garden, and in the garden a new tomb, and there they buried him. There we left him in our Good Friday commemoration. But on the evening of the third day after, he makes it known to the apostles that he is alive and with them, and they hear the voice say, 'Peace be unto you,' and at the word Peace they see the wounds of Calvary. The Easter faith is never to be separated from the challenge of the three Crosses. And one of the men who was near to our Lord on the hill of Calvary and among those to whom the revelation came on Easter evening, after many years of experience in the following of Jesus, wrote, or inspired another to write: 'This is the victory that overcomes the world, our faith.'

Abortion

I speak today[1] about the difficult subject of abortion. Almost a year ago the Church Assembly had a debate and passed this resolution:

> That the Assembly welcomes the Report *Abortion—An Ethical Discussion* because it stresses the principle of the sanctity of life for mother and foetus and urges the Church to preserve and demonstrate a balance between compassion for the mother and a proper responsibility for the life of the unborn child, and instructs the Board for Social Responsibility to continue its study of the subject.

Some confusion of procedure may at the time have seemed to weaken the force and authority of this resolution. It certainly has force and authority. Every phrase in it is important, and while different phrases will seem significant according to the angle from which they are viewed I would say that from the angle of a great deal of contemporary discussion a most significant phrase is 'the sanctity of life for the foetus', as it is this which is often either denied or passed by.

The emphasis upon this phrase goes back to the Report *Abortion—An Ethical Discussion*. I quote one of its key passages:

> If we are to remain faithful to the tradition, we have to assert, as normative, the general inviolability of the foetus; to defend, as a first principle, its right to live and develop; and then to lay the burden of proof to the contrary firmly on those who, in particular cases, would wish to extinguish that right on the ground that it was in conflict with another or others with a higher claim to recognition. Only so, in fact, can we maintain the *intention* of the moral tradition, which is to uphold the value and importance of human life. For invariably in this discussion the question must arise, which life? (pp. 31–2)

[1] An address to the Convocation of Canterbury on 17 January 1967.

It is well that we should now remind ourselves of this statement of first principles because in the debates occasioned by two successive Bills dealing with the matter in the past year first principles have become somewhat obscured by the sheer mass of detailed discussion of how much or how little.

We know that some people desire legal facilities for abortion going far beyond any of the current proposals and would like to make abortion lawful virtually at will. If we remember that this is to revert to the state of things in the ancient world before Christianity it helps us to see what the role of Christianity has been in this matter. Lecky, describing the enhancement of the value of human life which Christianity brought, wrote this:

> The practice of abortion was one to which few persons in antiquity attached any deep feeling of condemnation. . . . In Greece Aristotle not only countenanced the practice but even desired that it should be enforced by law when population had exceeded its assigned limits. No law in Greece, or in the Roman Republic, or during the greater part of the Empire, condemned it. A long line of writers, both Pagan and Christian, represent the practice as avowed and almost universal. . . . It was probably regarded by the average Romans of the later days of Paganism much as Englishmen in the last century regarded convivial excesses, as certainly wrong but so venial as scarcely to deserve censure.[1]

Now when it brought its vastly enhanced view of the sanctity of human life, Christianity condemned both abortion and infanticide which had been widespread in the ancient world. In condemning both abortion and infanticide the Church from the time of Constantine virtually equated the two. Both were the destruction of life, both were murder. Though there was no invariable doctrine as to the point in time in which human existence with a soul was held to begin, yet the destruction of the foetus was the destruction of a life sacred to God and to man. From this there followed the absolutist principle in refusing any and every abortion as unlawful.

The authors of *Abortion—An Ethical Discussion*, and by implication the bishops, clergy, and laity who passed in the Church

[1] *History of European Morals* (1886), II, pp. 21–2.

Assembly the resolution which I quoted, stand by the belief that the human foetus is held to be sacred. It is indeed very hard to be certain how many days or weeks after conception the foetus is to be identified with a human personality. It is uncertain at what stage terms like 'person' or 'human being' should be used. It is thus misleading to identify abortion and infanticide: both devalue human life, but they are not identical and it is wrong to stir emotion by identifying them. Yet the authors of the Report continue, and I believe that we shall be right to continue, to see as one of Christianity's great gifts to the world the belief that the human foetus is to be reverenced as the embryo of a life capable of coming to reflect the glory of God whatever trials it may be going to face.

But does this mean the absolutist position against abortion? No, the absolutist position is strained to absurdity when it is seen that it can in certain circumstances condemn both the mother and the foetus to death,[1] and thereby pose the question: Should not the one *or* the other be saved if possible? This leads on to the view that the underlying principle, rather than the letter, of the older Christian tradition demands that there may be the choice between the life and mental and bodily health of the mother and the life of the foetus. There are occasions when the latter, which is an embryonic and potential life, may be sacrificed for the former which is a life already. That is the main contention of the Report. This possibility is already maintained in the case law of this country, and it is urged to make it explicit in the statute law.

Now what do we say about extensions of the law of abortion beyond this point? I should say we should approach every proposal with due weight to our belief in the sacredness of life, the life of the foetus and the life of the mother. I mention two particular proposals:

1. There is the proposal to make abortion lawful when two doctors agree 'that there is a substantial risk that if the child were born it would suffer from such physical or mental abnormalities as to be seriously handicapped'. Here is another principle. There are some important questions for us to ask. What is the degree of risk? We have been told in relation to the cases which are chiefly in view that the proposed law might involve the risk of

[1] Cf. *Abortion—An Ethical Discussion*, p. 27.

the destruction of five potential lives without the abnormality
as against the risk of one life with the abnormality. These
tragedies draw from us all the utmost thoughts of compassion.
Yet we do have to ask about this contrary risk. Nor can we
forget people who were born severely handicapped and have yet
been far more glad to be alive than dead. I understand that
gross deformity cannot with certainty be diagnosed until about
the thirteenth week of pregnancy and that then termination is
already permissible under the Infant Life (Preservation) Act
1929. Should we not rely upon this existing legislation until such
time as medical knowledge can tell us that there is far less risk
of the destruction of normal lives than the present wording of the
proposal would entail?

2. Then there is the proposal to allow termination of pregnancy
when 'the woman's capacity as a mother will be severely over-
strained by the care of a child or of another child'. Here too we
think of circumstances which draw out the sympathy of our hearts.
But our hearts have also been moved by homes and families
in which it is amidst the utmost difficulties that some of the most
splendid things in human nature have been seen, with some of
the characters without which the world would be the poorer.
Ought we to legislate that a decision of two doctors should have
these issues in their hands? Ought we to legislate as though the
grace and power of God in human lives did not exist?

It is considerations such as these which lead me to think it
was both wise and right for the authors of *Abortion—An Ethical
Discussion* to urge that in any legislation the following problems
should be dealt with *only* under the category of risk to the life or
mental or physical health of the mother: the risk of the birth of a
deformed or defective child; conception after rape; circumstances
when the bearing and rearing of the child would prove beyond
the total capacity of the mother.

In drawing the line where I have suggested that it should
be drawn, what are the decisive considerations? There is the
consideration of compassion. But to this must be added the
consideration of justice, as we try to weigh one set of rights
against another, and one set of risks against another. And
besides both compassion and justice there are the two Christian

convictions of which we must never lose sight. The first is that the eternal destiny with God in heaven, possible to every child conceived in the mother's womb, matters supremely. The second is that while we must strive to remove suffering we do not foreclose the ways in which in the midst of frustrations and handicaps some of the glories of human lives may be seen.

The Family

We are here tonight[1] because we believe that the family is one of God's best gifts to the world. Without the happiness and security of family life society becomes rotten. Last week our beloved Queen after twenty-five years of a most happy marriage spoke of family life and said: 'I am for it.' I hope all of us who are here tonight are 'for it'. But we need to think carefully about what it is that we are 'for' and why.

We who are Christians believe that the family is part of God's scheme of things. When men and women take part in the pro-creation of children they have the wonderful privilege of sharing in God's creation of human life, and they are called to do this in God's way. And God's way means that procreation takes place not anyhow but by a man and woman who are joined together in a lifelong union, a union in which they give themselves to one another until death parts them. That is the atmosphere of love and stability into which, in God's design, children are born. And having been born in a family they are loved, cared for, and protected, and they grow up in the freedom and discipline of mutual love and care for one another. So when children go out to take their part in the world their role in their own family is not left behind but lasts as a permanent part of their lives. The happiest families are not introverted and wrapped up in their own circle but outgoing as a part of the wider community.

The family today faces a scene of immense social change, and it often has to express its own unchanging character amidst conditions different from those of the past. One big change is that far more women are going out to work, and the roles of the man and the woman in the home may not be distinguished in all the same ways as in the past: both may be sharing in the washing-up and both may be sharing in the earning of the family income. And there may be long distances between home and

[1] This address was given in the Central Hall, Westminster, on 30 November 1972.

work. Such is the setting in which the family virtues have to be rediscovered and practised.

Then there is the frequent conflict of generations. More than in the past, the young are striking out into intellectual independence and revolt against tradition. The need is to help the young to discover that Christian morality is not a negative tradition of rules and prohibitions but an adventure of freedom in the unselfish service of God and neighbour.

So these immense changes of social scene bring strains on the family. And sometimes there is the further strain of very unsuitable housing, or the difficulty of getting any housing at all. If we care about the family, this should be high amongst our priorities of concern.

Then there are the strains due to what is called the sexual revolution. I hope we welcome the greater openness about sex, as I am sure the old puritanical idea that sex should always be hushed up was unwholesome and did harm. We must avoid a kind of backlash towards puritanism. But sex is the bond of a union between two persons in their totality as persons; that is its true meaning. And today we have to witness against all those influences which separate sex from human personality and treat it as an excitement on a sub-human plane. The commercial exploitation of sex is horrible, yes horrible.

Then there is the idea which some are proclaiming that the family is an outmoded institution and should be superseded by some other pattern of human relationships. I am sure we cannot meet this propaganda effectively by denunciations. Rather must we show that the family has its own unique role within a society based on justice, brotherhood, and the true freedom found in the service of God. Our concern for the family goes hand in hand with our concern for justice in the community of which the family is a part.

Above all there is the need for the most thorough education in the meaning of the family, and education from the earliest years. Christians will cherish an education about the family which is rooted in the truth about the family in God's design and purpose, an education in which human relationships are linked with the knowledge and service of God. But when people are not Christians, then what? There the need is for the best possible teaching based upon the natural law of morality, and in this connection I refer to the important work which is being done by the Social Morality Council of which the Roman Catholic Bishop Christopher Butler is President. I hope we shall support the efforts of the Social Morality Council to meet an important need within the educational scene. To do so does not belittle the paramount importance of specific Christian teaching where it can be given and received.

Far more must be done to help those who are getting married to realize what is meant by the covenant to a lifelong union, and to be ready for the problems of parenthood. I should deprecate the introduction of a unified system of legal preliminaries to marriage, as the existing provision for getting married after banns in church or after a licence from a surrogate gives the clergy a great opportunity to know the couple from the outset and to prepare them to understand better what marriage means. This procedure needs to be strengthened.

The forces which threaten the family are deep and widespread in our society, forces social and economic as well as moral. If we are wise we shall not concentrate on denunciations of evil in the sexual sphere but shall try to cope at every point with the sickness in society which leads to such evil. For us who are Christians there is no substitute for bringing men and women and children to the knowledge and love of God, and it is this which gives to the family its deepest meaning and strength. Let all of us in this way show that we are 'for it'.

Ian Ramsey

Three of Durham's great bishops were buried in the lovely medieval chapel of Auckland Castle: Cosin, Lightfoot, Westcott; and it is fitting that the ashes of Ian Ramsey lie near to them. It will not be surprising if history comes to remember Brooke Foss Westcott and Ian Ramsey as the two bishops who made the biggest impact upon the Durham community.

It is never easy to speak about a dear friend or a great man, and it is doubly hard to speak about one who was both.[1] I have known other men who had something of Ian's winning warmth of heart and others who had Ian's liveliness of mind; but I have never known one in whom the warm heart and the lively mind were so completely of one piece. That was the secret of his influence as a theologian. He cared intensely that theology should listen to other disciplines if it is to have something intelligible to say in the contemporary scene. He cared no less that those who speak about Christian faith should do so with sensitivity to the many who find faith hard or incredible. These gifts made Ian Ramsey nearly unique amongst the theologians of our time in winning the attention and respect of people trained in other kinds of mental discipline. And for Ian this outreach on the frontiers of faith could never be an intellectual process alone. It meant outgoing friendship with people of many professions, a ceaseless engagement of heart and mind alike, a ceaseless giving of himself.

So when Ian left the academic life of Oxford for the very different tasks of a Bishop of Durham there was, for all the vast change of scene, a striking continuity of work and character. In Durham it was quickly apparent that he cared greatly about the community and its problems and was thinking vigorously about them. Those who worked in the mines and the shipyards, trades-unionists and managers alike, those who took part in local

[1] This address was given at a memorial service in St Margaret's church, Westminster, on 17 November 1972.

government or education or medicine or the social services, saw in the Bishop one who understood and cared, with a concern for people as well as for ideas and causes. So there was a renewal in a fresh form of the historic link between the see of Durham and the community, for Ian had a sense of the past as well as the present, and he was never happier than when he welcomed crowds of visitors to the Bishop's historic home and showed them the memorials of his great predecessors.

Inevitably Ian Ramsey's leadership was reaching far beyond his own diocese. The work of the Doctrine Commission, the production of the report on education entitled *The Fourth R,* the work of other groups of his own creation, a succession of speeches in the House of Lords made with the weight of considerable knowledge—amid all this his impact as a Christian leader was growing, and it was a leadership of a kind which no one else could give. But a frightening problem began to appear.

Is it possible for one man to lead the pastoral work of a diocese with its outreach to the community and at the same time to be taking part in national affairs and at the same time also to conserve the work of study, reading, thought, and teaching? Not many bishops have tried to combine these three roles at once, and those who have tried know that survival is only possible if there is a rigorous discipline in excluding things which do not matter and limiting painfully the things which do. Alas, it was impossible for Ian to admit the advice and experience of those who know something of the problem, because it had become a deep and inseparable part of his character never to say No. And in the office which he held, never to say No means before long to lose the power of discrimination and to be living in a whirl of mental and physical movement. The whirl became the whirlwind which swept Ian, like Elijah of old, to Paradise.

Yet perhaps if it were otherwise Ian would not be Ian. Perhaps the saying of No to any request of a fellow human being and the planning of priorities for himself were impossible for one to whom any incidental encounter, any person met, could be a thrilling disclosure, a bursting forth of one of God's secrets. Such was the man, with mind and heart ceaselessly engaged with people and ceaselessly engaged with truth and ready for truth to break out anywhere in a blaze of glory. That was the Ian God gave to us, and we are thanking God today for one of the best of his gifts that we have known, a gift not like any other. Our loving prayers surround Ian's brave family at this time, and for Ian we pray that he will now have the vision which our Saviour promised to the pure in heart.

Geoffrey Fisher

His servants shall serve him and they shall see his face.
Revelation 22.3

The passing of Geoffrey Fisher, who was for sixteen years our Archbishop and Primate, from the world where he had so long served Christ, the Church, and the people stirs in all of us emotions of love for him and gratitude to Almighty God for him. We in Canterbury feel this in a special way,[1] for throughout the far-reaching labours of the Primacy he found nothing nearer to his heart than Canterbury, the city, the diocese, the parishes, the people. He had been born in a country vicarage, and he loved to visit parishes and to mingle with everyone in friendship. However busy he was he would never spare himself in helping a person who needed help and showing that there was nothing he enjoyed more.

Fisher's gifts of mind were remarkable. With a skill in administration equal to that of anyone in any walk of life in the country, he brought into administration that care for people which gave the tone to all his work. So he led the way in practical reforms in the Church, like the improvement of the worrying conditions for many of the clergy and their families, and the reshaping of the Church's Canon Law, and the taking of the first steps towards the sharing together of bishops, clergy, and laity in the Church's government. But history is likely to remember most of all the wider outreach of the Church of England during his time. By strenuous journeys overseas he helped the widespread Anglican Churches to be a closely knit family, and by some courageous and imaginative actions he gave immense impetus to the cause of Christian unity. Never was this more apparent than when in the last year of his Primacy he visited Pope John XXIII in the Vatican, a visit which has opened a door which will never close. Today Christians of every tradition, Orthodox, Roman Catholic,

[1] This address was given in Canterbury Cathedral on 20 September 1972, the date of the Archbishop's funeral at Trent in Dorset.

Anglican, Protestant, salute the memory of a leader and a friend. In this country the Coronation of our Queen was among his finest hours, and there we saw him less as the servant of the State than as the servant of God whose simplicity and sincerity carried the spiritual meaning of the ceremony into the hearts of thousands who watched and listened.

Fisher could be outspoken when he was roused on any issue of public righteousness. But while he was sometimes stern he could never be pompous, for his humour led him to laugh about most things and often to laugh about himself. Controversy and obstinacy would sometimes melt before his acts of outgoing kindness. At the root of his character and his amazing industry was the simplicity of his faith in God.

Today lovely memories come crowding back of the days when he was with us, the days when he fed us with a faithful and true heart and ruled us prudently with all his power. We thank God for those days. And we thank God that now Geoffrey Fisher has gone beyond strains and shadows into joyful light, nearer to the perfect vision where God's servants shall serve him and shall see his face.

Nc

Church and State in England

Establishment has never been one of my enthusiasms. My knowledge of the Anglican Communion throughout the world has given me an admiration for the family of Anglican Churches amongst which the Provinces of Canterbury and York alone have established status. Recent history has seen the disestablished Church in Wales vigorous in its life and far from lamenting its loss of State privileges some fifty years ago. My own Nonconformist ancestry on my father's side gives me a feeling for that tradition of religion in this country which has for three centuries witnessed to Christ without the protection of privilege and can say 'at a great price obtained I this freedom'. Lastly, it seems that in the world as a whole Christianity is passing into a post-Constantian phase in which the buttressing of Churches by privilege may hinder rather than commend their witness and claim. It would not be grief to me to wake up and find that the English establishment was no more.

This is not to deny that the Church–State link in England has had much value in the past. It has meant some recognition of Christianity by the State, and it has helped the Church to be theologically comprehensive and to be pastorally involved with the whole community and not only with gathered congregations. Furthermore, it is difficult to dig up complex historical roots, and a programme of disestablishment in England would be an immense administrative operation, the outcome of which would be valuable only if the Church knew positively on what course it was moving. Disestablishment is itself a negative formula. It says what should be discarded. It would be better to ask: *quo tendimus?* What is it desired that the Church should *do* and *be* different from what it does and is at present? If the doing of it calls for the altering of parts, or the whole, of the State relationship, then we should be ready to pay the price.

Indeed, establishment is not any one and single 'thing'. It is a complex of laws and customs concerning the role of the Sovereign, the coronation of the Sovereign (which there would be a widespread desire to retain), the role of the bishops, the methods of church legislation, the privileges of the clergyman in his pastoral office, and a score of other phenomena. What does the Church imperatively require for its divine mission, and what are the hindrances to this? What burdens should it rightly accept in its Christian service of the State and the community? Not least, what changes does the cause of church unity in this country require? This last question cannot honourably be neglected, and the problems are not for us Anglicans to answer by ourselves alone.

Considerable reforms in the Church, for instance in the sphere of patronage and the distribution of the clergy, could probably happen without trenching upon the State relationship. I was disappointed that the more thoroughgoing solutions of those problems were not followed at the time of crucial decision in 1969. There are, however, two major issues, one (at the time when I write this) hopefully near to solution, and the other more delicate, which involves larger Church and State issues. The one is the power of the Church in its lawful ordering of its worship, and the other is the mode of the appointment of bishops. Both subjects were central in the work of the most recent Commission on Church and State, which was presided over by the Reverend Dr Owen Chadwick, Regius Professor of History in the University of Cambridge, and issued its report in 1970.

The history of the Church of Scotland shows that there has been no inherent impossibility in an established Church possessing autonomy in the ordering of its worship and in much else besides. In Scotland, however, the laity have long had a share in the government of the Kirk, and the Kirk has been recognizably homogeneous in its religious character and broadly representative of the greater part of Scottish Christianity. It is for those reasons that in Scotland establishment and autonomy have not been too difficult to combine. In England, however, the Church's own organs of government, where they have existed, have been in the past highly clerical in character; and the prestige of the bishops was once both considerable and often suspected. And it has been claimed with some justice that the role of the State in relation to the English Church has protected its comprehensiveness and prevented the ascendancy at any period of some one-sided theological movement. It has therefore been an assumption from history that if the established Church of England is to enjoy freedom in the ordering of its worship a necessary pre-condition is its possession of organs for self-government in which the laity share effectively along with the bishops and the clergy. It was not until 1970 that this came about.

A state of crisis meanwhile had been created by the rejection by the House of Commons in 1927 and 1928 of the Revised Prayer Book which the Convocations and the Church Assembly had approved by large majorities. After the rejection a note of challenge was struck by the bishops of the Provinces of Canterbury and York in the famous declaration which was read to the Church Assembly on their behalf by the cautious Archbishop Randall Davidson:

> It is a fundamental principle that the Church—that is the bishops together with the clergy and the laity—must in the last resort, when its mind has been ascertained, retain its inalienable right, in loyalty to our Lord and Saviour Jesus Christ, to formulate its Faith in Him and to arrange the expression of that faith in its forms of worship.

Could this, in the light of 1927 and 1928, be secured within the frame of the establishment, and how? One distinguished bishop of the time, Hensley Henson of Durham, was convinced that it could not, and 'burned his ships' for disestablishment.[1] Another distinguished bishop, Charles Gore, who had retired from the see of Oxford in 1919, had already reached the view that establishment was harmful to the cause of the Christian religion.[2] But counsels of patience prevailed in the ensuing years.

It would be tedious to recall here the steps which the Church took, after the 1928 rebuff, to find some way of securing autonomy within the establishment. The Commission presided over by Viscount Cecil of Chelwood proposed in 1935 a procedure for giving the Church considerable new autonomy. But no progress was made, partly because the Church's organs of self-government were insufficiently developed, partly because the heat of the 1927-8 controversy had not yet subsided, and partly because the approach of war in Europe soon caused other preoccupations to

[1] Cf. H. H. Henson, *Retrospect of an Unimportant Life* (1942–50), 2, ch. 15.
[2] C. Gore, *The Holy Spirit and the Church* (1924), p. 357.

supervene. When the theme of the Church's powers was resumed after the war, the Commission over which Sir Walter Moberly presided produced in 1952 no more than the very mild and moderate proposal that authority should be obtained from Parliament for the sanctioning by the Church's bodies of experimental forms of service alternative to those of the Prayer Book for periods up to fourteen years.

It was my privilege to introduce the Prayer Book (Alternative and Other Services) Measure into Parliament in March 1965, and this Measure followed the Moberly proposals. It enabled the Church to enjoy the lawful authorizing and use of services which have become familiar in recent years, the Series 2 and Series 3 services of Holy Communion amongst them. Prayer Book revision thus became a fact, and with it liturgical renewal of a kind most significant for the Church. But in the enjoyment of this it was not always realized that the powers which enabled this would expire round about the year 1980. Then, unless further powers were obtained, or the unthinkable course of taking a new Prayer Book to Parliament was followed, only the 1662 Book would remain lawful.

The Chadwick Commission accordingly recommended that the nettle of asking for new and greater powers should be grasped. Meanwhile the introduction of fully integrated Synodical Government in 1970 had provided a stronger background for this new step. So there followed the Worship and Doctrine Measure of 1974 which seeks for the Synod power to sanction forms of worship for any length of time. The Measure is a full and frank realization of autonomy within an established Church in England. It is being followed by a new Canon which uses the new Synodical powers to revise the form of Subscription to the Formularies, so that it will be more than ever clear that the clergy accept the Thirty-Nine Articles as a statement of the Church's historical position and not as a doctrinal definition for literal subscription. The gain for intellectual integrity and for tender consciences will be great, and so will the advantages for discussions with the Eastern Orthodox Church.

There is in the Measure one restrictive provision. The services of the Book of Common Prayer remain lawful, and any parish which, through the Parochial Church Council, desires to use any of them has the right to do so. I believe, myself, that this provision, which some would have liked to abolish, is the necessary condition for the privileged position of the Church in relation to the State. If the State gives privilege to one particular Church, it must know the identity of that Church—in this case a Church that is definable Anglican and not one which might decide at will to be Calvinist or Lutheran or Roman Catholic. The place of the Prayer Book as a *visible* standard, which may be used when it is asked for, is a mark of the Church's identity. Our Church in the matter of privileges cannot have it both ways. If total freedom is desired, the cost of it must be faced. But the Measure seems to represent what the Church has, unitedly and overwhelmingly, desired.

The bishops of the Church of England are nominated by the Sovereign on the advice of the Prime Minister. In the case of *suffragan* bishops there is a convention that the cleric who is the first to be named in the Petition presented by the diocesan, with the commendation of the Archbishop, is nominated. In the case of *diocesan* bishops there is no convention of a similar kind.

In recent years the restlessness in the Church about the system has increased considerably, not I think because of any marked disapproval of recent appointments but because of a feeling that the choice *ought* to be in the Church's own hands. The Chadwick Report deprecated a system of *diocesan* election of bishops, and recommended the bringing of a *provincial* body into the process of selection. But the Commissioners were divided between those who wished such a body to submit names for the Prime Minister to choose from and those who wished such a body to by-pass the Prime Minister and itself make a submission of a name to the Crown. The latter suggestion inevitably raises the constitutional question: Could the Sovereign act except on the advice of her chief Minister? and, perhaps still more, could the Sovereign nominate to an office involving membership of the House of Lords except on the Prime Minister's recommendation? In deciding whether to ask for one of the compromise solutions or whether to ask for election of bishops, pure and simple, the Church will have to ask itself what price it wishes to pay. In a word, does it care so much for making its own choice of its bishops as to be ready to see their place as peers of Parliament dropped?

I was very sorry that the Chadwick Report did not probe into the question of the value and importance of the bishops' contemporary role in the House of Lords. It was a strange and regrettable omission. I believe that their role there is valued and that it has influence, while it is very exacting for the time and energy of those who are ready to participate, whether in the general debates on Motions or in the Committee Stage of Bills, where sometimes the most crucial decisions of the House are made. Without presuming to know the answer, I wish that the Commission had explored how far membership in the House of Lords is the most suitable and effective forum for the bishops' influence in moral and social questions today. It will be remembered that while some spiritual peers, such as Garbett and Bell, made considerable use of the House of Lords as a medium, William Temple—who is often upheld as a kind of exemplar of the Church's prophetic witness—took very little part in the Lords throughout the years of his membership.

My own reading of history, and my experience of the system of Crown appointments during eighteen years as an archbishop, have led me to realize that its mode of operation has changed a good deal during the past half century and more. At the beginning of the century the Sovereign participated considerably in the discussions about the choice of a bishop; and Sovereign, Prime Minister, and Archbishop might throw names to and fro. Then came a period when the Prime Minister himself did the bulk of the work from the stores of his own considerable knowledge, with the leisure to give to the matter. Asquith's biographers thus describe his own procedure, quoting from one of his private secretaries who assisted him in this field:

He always showed the keenest interest in making Church appointments, and on ecclesiastical matters there can have been few laymen as well informed as he. He was well acquainted with past ecclesiastical history, had heard from his youth up many of the chief pulpit orators preach, and was on terms of friendship with many leading ecclesiastics and knew about the personalities and characteristics of very many more. He had little or no sympathy with the extreme High Church points of view, as he was by temperament and upbringing strongly Protestant in feeling, retaining until the close of his life what many would regard as an old-fashioned antipathy to the Roman Catholic Church. This Protestant bias, however, did not in any way affect his determination to select for Church appointments the persons he thought most suitable for the particular bishopric, deanery or canonry to be filled. It was my duty to put before him a short list of the persons considered most suitable for any particular post, and he weighed their respective claims with the most scrupulous care; and while he was always ready to receive the advice of the Archbishop of Canterbury, with whom he was very intimate, it was inevitably on his own unbiased selection that a name was submitted to the King. . . . In making selections he always attached, if not preponderating, yet very great importance to academic distinction, and I remember that he felt particular pleasure in nominating Dr Inge for St Paul's, thereby restoring the tradition that the holders of this position should be eminent scholars.[1]

I quote this account of Asquith's procedure not because I see it as an ideal, but because it needs to be realized how far the subsequent departures from such procedure have been and how far the departures have left lacunae to be filled in one way or another. Here was a Prime Minister with leisure to make his own study of ecclesiastical matters and to have many conversations on the subject with leading churchmen, with some of whom he was intimate, so that not only the decision but much of the background knowledge and spadework was his own. Nothing resembling this has occurred in recent years. But with the decline in the Prime Minister's own leisure, knowledge, and opportunity (though amongst subsequent Prime Ministers Macmillan had something of the older 'atmosphere'), how was the gap to be filled? It seems that there came a period when the Archbishop's views and suggestions counted for more, and that the convention whereby the Archbishop submitted three names for the Prime Minister's consideration grew in the years between the wars. It seems also that the Archbishop's influence was probably at its greatest in the primacy of Cosmo Lang and the earlier years of Fisher. But meanwhile Prime Ministers needed help from their own side of the Thames, and while civil servants had always

[1] J. A. Spender and Cyril Asquith, *The Life of Henry Herbert Asquith,* II, pp. 376–7.

assisted them, the new phenomenon was the highly competent and officially designated Appointments Secretary known as such to the Church at large as the man concerned.

I have indeed admired the conscientiousness with which Prime Ministers study the advice put before them and make their decisions. And I have never not admired the thoroughness with which the adviser explores the needs of a diocese and sifts the evidence, and the sympathy with which he has looked at the work and character of men to be considered. It is likely that with such a system there will be many sound nominations, likely also that there may from time to time be an inspired nomination like that of Ian Ramsey to Durham. It is also certain that there will be strange 'non-appointments' and chances missed—for the knowledge is filtered through the mind of one man, and no man is without his prejudices and blind spots. I do not doubt that divine providence can use the procedure, and that the bishops who are consecrated receive the gifts of the Holy Spirit for their office. But when all this has been said the system leaves me sharing the view that this is not the right way for any Church's chief pastors to be chosen.

It belongs, I believe, to the maturity and spiritual health of a Church that it should choose its own chief pastors, and a Church which is without such powers is warped in its potentiality of growing, through whatever hazards and mistakes, in the practice of Christian wisdom. Overseas, I have seen how the relinquishment of 'Canterbury' appointments in favour of election by the particular Church is a part of the process of maturity, and I do not know why the English Provinces should be different.

I add a few words on an aspect of episcopacy which is seldom discussed. There are the appointments, there are the non-appointments—and there are also the refusals, those who say *nolo episcopari*. History will notice the refusals as well as the appointments in the past decades. I believe that the Church must consider not only how it wants bishops to be appointed, but also how to use the bishop's office in such a way that men of some of the kinds which are greatly needed are not reluctant to accept.

The presence within the episcopate of *some* men who are leaders in thought and in the gift of theological exposition is urgent, not only for the sake of a kind of facade, but for two definite reasons. One reason is that if the House of Bishops is to give respected leadership in the counsels of the Church, its own counsels will contain, within its own number, a stock of learning on which to draw without having to look outside for it. The other reason is that more of the theological guidance needed by the clergy and the people amidst the contemporary strains upon belief should come from within the episcopate itself. The gap between church leadership and professional theology can grow only with grievous loss to both.

The gifts of God are still plentiful, and it must be our prayer that the Church will have the gift of wisdom to use them as it should. In both of the matters which this essay has discussed it should be possible to find both autonomy for the Church and a continuing partnership with the State.

Becket

Here we have no continuing city, for we seek one to come.

Hebrews 13.14

We have all come here today[1] to commemorate a man who had a place in the hearts of English people probably for a longer period of time and over a wider extent of the population than any other figure in our history. It is safe to say that no monarch or statesman or soldier or divine meant so much to so many English people through three and a half centuries as Thomas meant through the years from the Henry who did penance at his tomb to the Henry who destroyed it. It suffices to recall that when Chaucer wished to depict a nation in its lovely variety of character and colour he needed to look no further than to the columns of pilgrims along the way to Canterbury,

> and specially from every shires end
> of Engéland to Canterbury they wend
> the holy blissful martyr fór to seeke
> that them hath holpen when that they were sicke.

If your name is Tom, or if you have a son named Tom, you can be sure that the popularity of the name in national consciousness owes more to Thomas Becket than it owes to Thomas surnamed Didymus in the Gospel story.

But what kind of man was he? It seems that the longer historians wrestle with this question the more uncertain their results become. True, there were as many as eleven accounts of Thomas written near to his own time; and together they give a mass of information about him. Yet they fail to give a sure picture of his inner character. One reason is that they were written in the glow of enthusiasm for a much loved martyr, and in that glow the rough and the dark features are easily hidden. And another reason is that Thomas himself left no personal letters to reveal

[1] Address given in Canterbury Cathedral on 15 July 1970 in the year of the eighth centenary of Thomas Becket's death.

his own heart and mind (and perhaps he wrote none), unlike, for instance, Anselm, who shows us his own inner life in letters of friendship, letters of spiritual counsel, and letters of self-scrutiny which it is still a joy to read. Yet why complain? It is not the raw material of character which makes a martyr what he is. Rather is it by a man's use of that raw material of character as he approaches death that a martyr is both made, and makes subsequent history take the course it does. It is about a death and an approach to death that we are thinking today.

Today, therefore, we need not linger on the drama of Thomas Becket's life. But we glance at it. We see the early friendship of King and Chancellor as together they share in policy and government and in boyish and hilarious companionship. We see, but we need not pause to assess, the quarrel between them: it was about the freedom of the clergy from the secular criminal courts, and if to a modern mind it seems that Becket's case was that of an unreasonable clericalism we remember that it was a tiny part of a struggle throughout Europe for the autonomy of the Church against the sometimes untrustworthy power of sovereigns. Then we see, alongside Becket's ruthlessness of word and action, the change which comes in his style and life as he passes from Chancellor to Archbishop, and the courtier and servant of the State gives place to the ascetic and the priest. So the drama moves on: the bitter quarrel, the exile of six years beyond the seas. But while this drama is exciting to watch, it is not this which reveals a saint, it is not this which wields power over three centuries of history. It is a death and the approach to a death which show the man and win the battle.

The issue was this. Thomas saw that, with the conflict developing as it did, the only weapon left to him for winning the conflict was death. He chose that weapon, he prepared himself to use it, he wielded it; and when he fell he conquered, and by dying he won what he could never win by argument or controversy or diplomacy. Dare we say that in seeing death as the weapon of victory Thomas caught something of the secret of Christ's victory on the hill of Calvary, the secret that it is by sacrifice that wrong is overcome? So it was that by his death and from his death on that 29 December Thomas exerted a power over his enemies, a power over men and women, a power over history, that no argument or controversy or diplomacy could

ever achieve. *In hoc signo vinces.* It was not only that the immediate
cause prospered and that King Henry presently was kneeling
in abject penitence at the martyr's tomb. It was that for centuries
to come Canterbury gives the world one more illustration of
the truth that it is by self-sacrifice that the good can prevail and
evil can be defeated.

That is the message of the stirring weeks of December 1170.
At the beginning of the month Thomas lands at Sandwich. The
road is lined by rejoicing people, who perhaps feel in some
half-conscious way that the cause of their father-in-God is
the cause of the people's rights. They dare to sing 'Blessed is
he that comes in the name of the Lord', and one of the chroniclers
likens Thomas's ride to the city to the Saviour riding into Jerusalem on Palm Sunday. But Thomas's own mind is declared in the
sermon he preaches on the next day, 2 December, in the cathedral.
His text is: 'Here we have no continuing city, for we seek one
to come.' It is of no earthly kind of victory that he is now thinking.
And at the end of the day one of his friends says to him: 'My
Lord, it matters not now when you depart hence, since today
in you Christ's bride has conquered: yea, Christ conquers,
Christ reigns, Christ rules.'

Across the centuries the martyrdom of Thomas speaks to all of
us who are Christians. It speaks to all of us, whatever our ecclesiastical allegiance may be; and we rejoice that Roman Catholics have
shared in this commemoration as well as Anglicans and members
of other communions, for despite the things which divide us
we are brother Christians, and the martyr speaks to us all. To
all of us the martyrdom says that we are called as Christians to
be loyal; loyal to our faith in the supernatural, loyal to our divine
Lord and Saviour, loyal to the saving power of his Cross. We are
called fearlessly to uphold what is right amidst the needs of the
times in which we are living. And the martyrdom also tells us
that in the upholding of what is right self-sacrifice can win
victories which violence and controversy can never win. Hard
as it is to grasp, and hard at times to apply in practice to particular circumstances, the way of the Cross is the way in which evil
is conquered. Furthermore, we hear Thomas's sermon here in
the cathedral, 'Here we have no continuing city, for we seek
one to come.' The message of the martyrdom is that we should
think far more than we sometimes do about heaven—heaven as

the goal of our calling, heaven as the true perspective of our present warfare and our present ideas of failure and success. What a difference it will make to our conflicts, our ambitions, our right and proper striving for God's kingdom in this world, if Thomas's text and Thomas's sermon are always in our hearts: 'Here we have no continuing city.'

And now the evening of 29 December is drawing on. Thomas has left the Old Palace. Where is he? Where is he? He is standing in the north transept. A shout is heard: 'Where is the traitor, Thomas Becket?' 'Here I am, no traitor, but a priest ready to suffer in my redeemer's cause. God forbid that I should flee from your swords, or depart from what is just. But do not touch any of my people.' And a little later: 'I accept death for the name of Jesus and for the Church.' He falls. *keito megas megalōsti.* 'Great he was,' says one of the chroniclers, 'great he was in truth . . . great when going forth on his pilgrimage, great when returning, and great at his journey's end.' Here we have no continuing city, for we seek one to come.